809
Sto

Stonier.
Gog Magog.

Date Due

GOG MAGOG

GOG MAGOG

AND OTHER CRITICAL ESSAYS

BY

G. W. STONIER

Essay Index Reprint Series

BOOKS FOR LIBRARIES PRESS, INC.
FREEPORT, NEW YORK

1966

84150

First published 1933
Reprinted 1966

Printed In The United States of America

CONTENTS

GOG MAGOG

A SMALL crowd had collected in Oxford Street to watch the builders. The huge metal framework, streaked with rust but cutting strongly into the sky, dominated the street. On either side, the buildings looked curiously dwarfed and ugly. A chain of workmen was passing bricks from one to another with an easy swinging movement: up the bricks swung, from hand to hand, story to story, ending on a dizzy platform aloft.

It was a delight to watch: the ritual of the men, the vast clean structure. In a few months this gaunt pattern would be muffled with brick, stone, and concrete; for a while there would be an entrancing criss-cross of wood and iron-piping meshed round walls and making a thousand delicate lines and cuts for the eye; then the nest is stripped off, the building stands out by itself, white and bland—another monument of banality! No crowd will stand to look at *that*. The smoke, mercifully, of the town will smudge it out till it looks as black as King's Cross Station.

Then people will be staring at other new buildings going up.

At the end of a street, in the corner of a square, one sees the same process—the half-dismantled building, with vacant windows and the wallpaper peeling off under the sky—men like alpinists balanced on summits and hacking away at the brick under them—the awkward loom of a crane, like a giant lobster, wheeling, clawing, and lifting rubbish. What a fascination it has, this ruthless pulling down, and the outlines of a new construction! The bared skeleton, fibre of workmanship! It is the *process* that fascinates; no one cares about the dilapidation that is being erased or the neutral efficiency that is taking its place. For the artist, at any rate, there is no beauty here of beginning or end, but only this intermediate beauty—the transition, the stir, the incompletion —the building half-way up or down, the ruin and the emergent pattern.

.   .   .

Everyone repeats as a truism that we live in an age of transition: only the artist perhaps realizes how deeply we are interested in the process of transition. How is this being done?—that is the vital question. Capitalism declines and some form of Communism will probably take its place —but we do not look forward to Communism, prepare for it or defend against it: we examine with an inexhaustible curiosity the changes in ourselves. Very odd! A Lord Mayor's procession jogs by, the band plays: there is a procession of the unemployed and a police charge. We look on, very interested. All this, we say, is *happening*. Now.

.   .   .

An age of transition, town-life, specialism, criticism, self-analysis.

.   .   .

There are no far horizons, no stretches or hill-curves, in towns. The chimney-pot leans close above you against a cloud. Raindrops dribble their pearl on bus windows. Down the wedge of a straight road you glimpse distance: a scissored piece of sky; the tide of faces. Night carves the street in granite.

.   .   .

The old trinity of the poet—God, man, and nature—has become now: the poet, the man-in-the-street, the street. Those are now the centres of stimulus.

.   .   .

The arts have turned in on themselves. In an age of self-scrutiny the artist strives not for achievement but for the revelation of the processes of creation (artistic creation). 'The only fiction worth while is that which deals unreservedly with the writer's self' (Strindberg). The emphasis now would be more on *the writer's* than on *self*.

.   .   .

Proust, first of the moderns, revealed the artist thinking, engrossed in his pattern, picking up here and there the threads of memory: or rather you see him with a vast sheet of paper spread out on which there is invisible writing, and on this paper he works the revealing chemical with

little dabs of his brush-point; first one, then
another corner shows.

.   .   .

Eliot, going a step farther, has dragged the roots
of his poetry into expression: the flower, too
often, must be imagined.

Joyce, too. *Ulysses* is a vast study of method.
Eliot and Joyce are concerned less with effect
than with means.   Themselves the poets of
transition, their work is transitional in its fibre:
at once nearer the springs of creation in the
poet's mind and farther from the achieved
expression to which we have been used in the past.

.   .   .

Hence the isolation of literature since the War:
Joyce, Eliot, Wyndham Lewis, even Lawrence,
are comparatively little read.   The separation
between what is literature and what is literary
entertainment has increased so that now there is
a real gulf, wider than ever before, between the
two.   One reason for this is the increasing
specialism of the writer.   Another is the decline
of the play-instinct: attempts, by Evreinov and
Cocteau, to reinstate it have been self-conscious
and brittle.

.   .   .

Is literature beginning, then, like music, to
develop into a 'pure' art, with meanings and
effects inseparably of its own? Or has it gone up
a temporary byway from which in more stable

times it will return? (But this involves a doubtful conditional.)

.   .   .

The present situation has obvious general causes: (1) the onslaught of scientific knowledge, (2) general acceptance of the findings of psychoanalysis, (3) disruptive effects of the War and the Bolshevik revolution.

.   .   .

(1) and (2). The more literature is abstracted from the *forms of action* and becomes psychological rather than formal, the more difficult it will be for the artist to use conventional art-forms. Proust, having an entirely feminine genius, was content with being an Oblomov in a musical world of the sensations, but writers since Proust who are equally psychological have already felt the need of stricter form. Eliot and Joyce are examples of the attempt of the masculine intelligence to make artistic form out of the chaotic flux of modern psychological 'truth'. Neither has wholly succeeded, though approaching the attempt from opposite sides, for in Eliot's skeleton poetry and Joyce's daydream prose the characteristic art-form is equally the phantasmagoria (*The Waste Land* and *Walpurgisnacht*). Compare the formal beauty of the medieval vision with the shapelessness of its modern equivalent, the dream or daydream psycho-analytically interpreted. The difficulty of the modern poet who is sensitive to his surroundings is that, rightly or wrongly, science has

smashed up the whole edifice of poetic imagery, so that for many people it no longer has meaning, and the only loophole left to the poet is a symbolism based on scientific fact and an exploration of the new mythology introduced into culture by the theories of the psycho-analyst. Psychoanalysis has taken the place of religion as a belief on which art (for the moment) can build: in a materialist world it alone offers an Unconscious in place of a soul, an egocentric universe in place of a cosmic one, a re-entrance into myth and legend. But it does not provide the artist with forms (as, for example, Christianity provided the early Italian painters with definite forms as well as belief and legend).

.   .   .

(3) Disruption has been of two kinds: (*a*) disruption of the individual personality (by psycho-analysis, by the lapse of religion, by the lack of belief in any system of morals, following the War); (*b*) social disruption—decay of the aristocracy, embarrassment of the bourgeois, fear of Communism. Both these types of disintegration, individual and social, are reflected and, indeed, to some extent, foreshadowed in literature. *Ulysses* and *The Waste Land* are works of disintegration which attempt a new formulation of attitude and of literary style.

.   .   .

Wyndham Lewis has said that all modern politics are revolutionary; the same is true of the arts. Even Lawrence appears revolutionary if he is compared with English novelists before him. He gives us a picture of life which seems to be the exact opposite of what we have come to expect of life in fiction; his characters live at precisely those moments which hitherto the novelist has avoided mentioning. (They begin by undressing.)

Lawrence and Dickens might be taken as complete opposites.

.   .   .

How rare it is to find a book of criticism which gives any recognizable graph of literary movements in England between 1880 and 1930! Obviously there has been a break somewhere. At most we learn that each age denies the attitude of the age immediately preceding it, and we are left with the impression that literature advances by a series of reactions, or swings of the pendulum. Such an explanation is of course superficial, because negative. Those critics who see in contemporary literature chiefly a recoil from Victorianism, to which in due time another generation will return, betray their own weakness: they have never themselves got further in imagination than the Victorian age.

.   .   .

At intervals certain forms of thought and sentiment die and are discarded: there is no more possibility of returning to them than of the snake getting back into its old skin. A masterpiece closes one avenue of thought for ever; the death-mask, final and unalterable, has been taken; to *that* an artist may return as to a Euclid problem. But besides these death-masks of great art, themselves living in fixity, there are the inferior death-masks imposed not by an artist but by a period—the attitudes and platitudes of the time. Every movement, at first springing and individual, undergoes in the end a popular disintegration. The impulse of Byron's poetry degenerates into Byronism—we may return to the first, but not to the second; tradition becomes traditionalism, and then, from the point of view of art, it is dead, discarded as useless.

.   .   .

With the Victorians a huge slice of tradition went rotten. Their books, like their houses, are full of a spurious ornament and furniture put in 'for the sake of the picture'. In art as in other things they made for solidarity, and the result, for us, is often superficial and false. To this extent our own literature is a reaction against Victorianism. Where the Victorians are 'easy' we are 'hard'. We have rejected the prettiness, the security of a buttressed convention. That poetry should be immediately intelligible, for example, and taken in at sight, was carried to a pitch of softness which we completely deny.

.   .   .

But the reaction has been against the whole tradition which ended in Victorianism. Looking back thirty, fifty, a hundred years, we are aware

of a gradual accumulation of case-law in literature; the characters of fiction belonging inevitably
to fewer and fewer types, the situations becoming
stereotyped; each word case-determined, for there
must be no new judgment, but only an occasional
addition to an old one; everywhere in books an
atmosphere of unreality as in a law court, a falsity
of tone extending over poetry, fiction, and essays.
Literature with an increasing bowdlerization had
reached the limit of a set of conventions in the
great Victorian novelists.   Their impulse was
spent in the creation of genre—how dead now
the surface of much of their writing appears! Any
activity outside the law was treated as bolshevik.
Hopkins, the sole revolutionary artist of the time,
was suppressed as unintelligible, and even Hardy's
pastoral scene shocked.

.   .   .

We had in England none of that volcanic
impulse which was breaking out in other parts
of Europe, no 'mad genius' comparable with
Strindberg, Nietzsche, Dostoevsky, or Van Gogh;
and consequently we missed the polarity of those
great pairs of genius, Ibsen and Strindberg,
Goethe and Nietzsche, Tolstoy and Dostoevsky,
whose opposition enlarged and vitalized the
whole of European thought.   Samuel Butler,
Wilde and the pessimists were the extent of our
madness; and they flattered complacency at the
same time that they pricked it. The Art for Art's
sake doctrine which had found its true expression

in Flaubert tailed off in the decadents of the
nineties : our 'plain-speaking' on sex was confined
to—Swinburne ! The Victorian position was
still being attacked by Shaw and defended by
Galsworthy up to the outbreak of the War.

.   .   .

We missed a vital step in the development of
literature, and our revolution, now that it has
come, has been the more complete and violent.
The influences have come from abroad.   For
Eliot, it was not the discovery of Donne or Dryden
that was important, but his early contact with
Laforgue.   His London 'the unreal city', reinforced by James Thomson and Dante, takes us
back to Paris in the sixties. The lag is irreparable ;
no amount of virtuosity can cover it up or lessen
its bad effect on other and younger poets. Joyce
has learned chiefly from Flaubert; but here there
has been a natural development of important
tendencies latent in the European novel (and
unheard of in England) for fifty years. *Ulysses* is
not the dead-end that *The Waste Land* is.

.   .   .

The type of genius at the end of the last
century was the *madman* ; now it is the *invalid*.

.   .   .

Proust's avenue of bed-dreams.
Eliot's pessimism of a marionette.
Joyce's mental tic.

.

This art, ingrained, intent on itself—an art not being, but becoming—shows a curious mixture of activity and inaction. Atoms spinning in an immense recumbent hulk—the Oblomovism of modern letters. The gigantic sprawl of Proust's novel and of *Ulysses*—both bed-bound in the imagination.

. . .

An atmosphere of the sickroom spreading over literature. Much criticism at the present time is diagnosis. From this new angle literature appears as a disease of great or sensitive minds, expression as a purge or at any rate a symptom; and the critic arms himself with stethoscope and knife. It is not difficult to gauge the clinical atmosphere of Proust: from Proust to Dostoevsky is a short step, richly rewarded. And when once a start has been made, what is to prevent the investigator from going back to Shakespeare, Lamb, and Johnson, and applying his diagnostics there? Shakespeare's homosexuality, Lamb's drunken sentiment, even Johnson with his twitchings and orange-peel, make first-rate 'cases'. Does this seem exaggerated?

. . .

A medical historian has stated recently, as the result of elaborate researches, that in the whole of literature he can find only one man—Sir Walter Scott—whom he would describe as perfectly sane. Freud and Jung have shown how an artist's or a poet's creations may be used as evidence against

him—evidence that cannot lie! Professor Kretsch-
mer, in an introductory volume to a vast and
important work on the nature of genius, has
reached the conclusion that genius is inseparable
from psychosis; and he examines the lives not
only of great writers, artists, and musicians, but
of men of all kinds to whom the word genius is
commonly applied. His argument, though
extreme, is formidable. In itself it shows the
way the wind is blowing.

.   .   .

Few of us, however serene our approach, can
investigate the writings of Proust, of Joyce or
Eliot, without some clinical excitement, some
thrill of the probe. We seem to discover in them
reflections of our own ills. Their work is the
product of a gigantic dissatisfaction, hardly concealed by lavish sensibility. We approach it with
equal dissatisfaction, with the idea that *something
is wrong*, that at the core of this astonishing
display of sensibility there is a complex to be
unravelled. What is this worth as literature?
seems much too easy a way of looking at it.

.   .   .

The important fact about any work of art is
not whether its author is mad or sane, but whether
his art is.

.   .   .

Perhaps the most interesting diagnosis of
modern letters is to be found in Wyndham

Lewis's *Time and Western Man*. He insists there, it will be remembered, on a time-obsession inhibiting modern writers and their work; even the Stein stutter is attributed to the influence of the clock. I have no space here to examine his criticism in detail, but as it applies to Proust (an obsession with the past) and Joyce (a fixation of the present) there is obviously much truth in it. Another aspect of their work strikes me more forcibly (this applies less to Proust) : the aspect of *size*. The failures in *Ulysses* are due surely to some dislocation of the author's sense of size. It is not merely that the characters and the world they live in change stature as the book moves from one section to another—Bloom at one moment is the conscious hub of the universe, at another he is a pinprick in the past ages of literary history. These changes of size bewilder, and rob the book of unity. But even more, there is a nightmare horror of mere size in itself—the infinitely large, the minutely small—such as children experience often in dreams, before presumably they have adjusted themselves to the scale of the universe; and this horror of size in *Ulysses*, absence of the norm, is increased by the magnification and diminishing of objects for which Joyce can find no constant perspective. To a modern physicist man is an atom in a universe of stars; to the psycho-analyst he is a boundless consciousness containing universes of his own; and between these two conceptions—the outer pigmy and the inner giant—it is possible for the mind to invent the most distorted visions. Joyce, it seems to me, possesses such a mind. Sex is for him at once a bottomless hell and a dirty joke. He labours to see the mind with a granular closeness—but its thoughts when seen are exhibited with contempt. Even his sense of farce, which comes nearest to banishing the nightmare, leaves the characters in *Ulysses* still distorted. They are rarely more than painting, here a quiet interior, there a surrealist jumble of impressions—a number of planes superimposed but still at odds: they rarely have the depth or shading of sculpture. In his recent *Work in Progress* Joyce seems at last to have discovered a world of the subconscious—night-self to the day-self of *Ulysses*—where the creatures are related in a constant perspective; but in discovering it, to have lost coherence.

. . .

The focus in *Ulysses* is on the page. Held by that difficult and changing verbal magic, the reader may at first hardly notice the nightmare beyond. One can read the book as a new *Anatomy of Melancholy*, and enjoy, as one critic has put it, this 'banquet of the modern consciousness' without qualm. But look beyond the words, and the horror and shifting uncertainty of Joyce's vision is plain. He has no fixed attitude (as even Proust, for instance, has).

. . .

Illness. You see people every day running for trains and buses. The normal rhythm does not

impress you: when you look attentively, it is
because the running figure is somehow eccentric.
I remember seeing a man who was slightly lame
running a few yards along the street to catch a
postman who was clearing a letterbox. The lame
foot dragged a little as though it were a weight
pulling at all the nerves and tendons of the body.
The rhythm of this lame man running was so plain
and striking that one unconsciously transformed
him into a pattern—a moving pattern of wiry
energy—weighted always by the pivot of his
dragging foot.

The rhythm of much modern art depends on a
dragging foot. We have ceased to notice the
normal motions of the body.

.   .   .

Literature is discussed in terms of sensibility.
So-and-so (the critics say) has enlarged our
sensibility, widened the possibility of our experience. (The emphasis is on individual values,
in contrast to the social drama and fiction of the
period before the war.)

The charabanc, the aeroplane, and the movie
have equally 'enlarged our sensibility'.

.   .   .

Sensibility, of course, should be the means,
and not the objective, of art.

.   .   .

The highest point of consciousness is always
the present. Looking back in history, we are
aware of a diminishing consciousness like the

perspective of a road. As literature recedes into the past it becomes more objective; seen rather than felt. How far this is due to natural perspective, how far exaggerated by the fact that consciousness was indeed more limited in earlier ages, is impossible to determine.

We have seen into, and through, things.

.   .   .

The War knocked a hole in our public statues, and the sawdust has trickled out. But the empty shells remain: the country houses belonging to peers who have gone in for journalism, the churches which must be 'preserved' though never filled, the politicians, looking like President Harding or Trafalgar Square lions, who are less real than their caricatures. Little groups of resisters band together to plant trees and to preserve rustic views; but the new roads, the bungalows and the spreading of towns go on. All this is reflected in literature. The time-honoured phrases are empty. The vices and the virtues, the plot and the moral, the 'solid' figures you can see round, have gone out of fiction. The Romantic stuffing has been knocked out of poetry; and with it much of the impulse, too, has gone.

> We are the hollow men,
> We are the stuffed men.

Even our revue-writers are up against a blank.

> Dance, dance, dance, little lady
> —So obsessed
> With second-best.

.   .   .

The message of Eliot's poetry—so far as it has one—is Amen to life and Good-bye, with rather more lingering, to art. The afterglow of a gas-fire turned out. Soon all is dark. (So at least one supposes.)

.   .   .

Everywhere there are difficulties. It is difficult (we are told)

> for the poet to write poetry
> for the reader to read poetry

but of course it 's still easy enough to print in spite of high prices. Let us take two writers, a poet and a critic, well in the van of literature: Eliot and I. A. Richards. Eliot's poetry is an anthologizing ('these fragments shored against my ruin') which is often in effect literary criticism, since it represents an attitude to literature rather than to life, and since it is the product, not of impulse, but of taste. Richards, the head of a new school of criticism, is a critic, not of literature, but of criticism. He has written little about creative literature worth preserving.

Here, then, we have a poet who is really a critic, and a critic who is only a critic of other critics. The new puritanism.

.   .   .

I. A. Richards: 'Criticism will justify itself as an applied science when it is able to indicate how an advertisement may be profitable without necessarily being crass'.

Eliot: Because I know that time is always time
And place is always and only place
And what is actual is actual only for one time
And only for one place
I rejoice that things are as they are and
I renounce the blessèd face
And renounce the voice
Because I cannot hope to turn again
Consequently I rejoice, having to construct something
Upon which to rejoice.

.   .   .

This passage, according to a young satellite critic, is 'the pith of the whole of Mr. Eliot's poetic message. It is the fearless, the truly modern thought behind it that is influencing many of our better young poets for their good'—consequently I rejoice.

.   .   .

Eliot eavesdrops on life. With an imagination rooted in literature, he keeps one slightly deaf ear open to what is going on round him: the dull voices at tea-parties, a honk from the street, the photographs in the newspapers. One eye notices with a curious flatness the typical corners of London. Into this *News-of-the-World* world he projects the commonplace half of himself, a J. Alfred Prufrock, an 'Apeneck' Sweeney, like the comics in a seaside film; 'and cries Jug, jug to dirty ears'.

.   .   .

The poet and the man-in-the-street. Eliot—

Prufrock ; Joyce—Bloom ; Flaubert—Bouvard and
Pécuchet.

Inevitably one goes back to Flaubert.

Madame Bovary—with the cry 'Pas de monstres
et pas de héros !'—was the bible of most English
and French novelists of importance open to
new influences at the end of the nineteenth
century. Turgenev, Zola, Maupassant, Henry
James, George Moore, Anatole France, Proust—
to name only a few—were deeply indebted to
Flaubert. Strange that one book should have
been so variously interpreted (such message as it
has is for artists), that a phrase here and a scene
there should have been the starting-point of
writers, many of whom had little in common
with Flaubert or with one another. Reading the
book now we are proof against surprise, but the
more capable perhaps of understanding Flaubert's
certainty. It is not merely that *Bovary* remains a
masterpiece, clearer in its perfection to-day than
ever before ; nor that it anticipates so many books
written since, and indeed discounts them in
advance : it is that we find ourselves exclaiming
again and again as we read : 'He 's *right*. There,
in that paragraph and that word, Flaubert
proves he is right. Given the conditions, a novel
must be written like that'. Beside this certainty
of Flaubert's, in which as a novelist he is unique,
Henry James's 'point of view' or Proust's time-
map are the most arbitrary of conventions.

Among comparable writers Tolstoy possessed greater genius than Flaubert, but his influence on novelists, except superficially, has been far less. Nevertheless it would be wrong to attribute Flaubert's influence to a mastery of technique only, to his infallible gift of method, for his attitude to life as much as to literature has infected those who followed him.

If *Madame Bovary*, *L'Education Sentimentale* and to a smaller degree *La Tentation de Saint Antoine*, were key-books of the later nineteenth century, we must look now to *Bouvard et Pécuchet* and the *Correspondance* for the attitude of contemporary writers.

.　　　.　　　.

It is an attitude of pessimism in a rising tide of folly—pessimism backed by artistic certainty. Flaubert never doubted his art or the great art of the past; he knew—and he was right—that art, an art increasingly influenced by science, was the only bulwark of culture against a stupid democracy. 'La bêtise', he wrote in a letter in 1874, 'entre dans mes pores.' And in another letter: 'O France! Bien que ce soit notre pays, c'est un triste pays, avouons-le! Je me sens submergé par le flot de bêtise qui le couvre, par l'inondation de crétinisme sous laquelle peu à peu il disparait. Et j'éprouve la terreur qu'avaient les contemporains de Noé, quand ils voyaient la mer monter toujours. Les plus grands bénisseurs, tel que le père Hugo, commencent eux-mêmes à douter'. (Pessimism has

gone some degrees further since Flaubert.) In
reply to a letter from George Sand in 1875
rallying him on his preoccupation, he wrote:
'Ne me dites plus que "la bêtise est sacrée comme
toutes les enfances", car la bêtise ne contient
aucun germe'. A large part of his life was
devoted to the discovery and registration of the
commonplace-comic; as a youth of nineteen, the
author of heroic plays and a history of the world,
he was already collecting the clichés of guide-
books during a walking-tour in the Pyrenees.
The famous *Dictionnaire des Idées Reçues* and the
Sottisier, gathered at all periods of his life, remain
(in the hands of the French government) un-
published. *Bouvard et Pécuchet*, an unfinished epic
of the commonplace, based on the two *dossiers*
and considered by Flaubert to be his masterpiece,
was published posthumously.

      .   .   .

Pessimism, I have said, has gone far since
Flaubert—I mean, of course, artistic pessimism,
for we live in a world of roaring optimists who
even in depression outvie Pangloss. When
Bouvard et Pécuchet was written (1872–80) the
bourgeois world was still pretty solid, and
stupidity still more or less native and in its
infancy. Flaubert got his *sottises* not only from
conversation and newspapers but from innumerable books on science, theology, medicine, garden-
ing, history, literature, and philosophy: he chose
the best authorities, and it was big-game hunting

in rich country.   Since then the animals have all
learnt their tricks, at the crack of the business
and newspaper whip, and when the huntsman
approaches, instead of turning tail or showing
fight they sit up (puppets of the modern circus!)
and beg.   The Bouvards and Pécuchets of the
modern age, tame and knowing, rattled by jazz
and galvanized in the limbo of the wireless world,
have been transformed from private individuals
into public heroes.   *Every man a hero* in this best
of best possible worlds!   So the new Everyman,
'Mister Everyman', Prince Charming of the
business fairy-tale, in search of nothing but a piece
of furniture, strides into the Drageway palace to
be met by his kind old uncle, or into the picture
palace for screen kisses, or into the gin-palace
(there 's a touch of the blackleg here) to forget
the world.   Bouvard and Pécuchet have found
their Alf's button at last, for here is a heaven
below their understanding in which no man can
help being king.

                    .   .   .

Direct satire of such a world being next to
impossible, the realistic artist can either give in
(like Joyce) or resist (like Wyndham Lewis).   We
have the results in *Ulysses* and *The Childermass*,
both epics of the commonplace, the one sympa-
thetic, the other pantomime : both springing from
the later Flaubert.

                    .   .   .

Bouvard and Pécuchet, in their search for

knowledge, remained comic and *ordinary*, because
the landscape about them was solid, the moonlight lay still on the cornfields round their extraordinary garden and the house with its tapestry,
altar, and dissected corpse. *Pas de monstres et pas
de héros*—the comic pair were neither. They are
Everyman figures because of their very *smallness*,
as the figures before them—Quixote, Falstaff,
Pantagruel—are universal through being great.
Flaubert achieved an extraordinary creation with
these small figures and a still landscape, and the
comedy of human knowledge. Joyce and Lewis,
taking up the same theme, isolating the man-in-
the-street, keeping his bowler-hat and his mental
stock of press-clippings, find the figures eluding
them, growing ominously large; the landscape
loses focus and becomes a kaleidoscope; and the
comedy of human knowledge!—ah, that detachment, too, has gone, lost in the roar of a bus-top,
the wind round the corner. As they zig-zag
towards us in the half-light, traditional back-chat
comedians, the Gog and Magog of a neighbouring
pub or lamp-post encounter, we see that their
very ordinariness has become monstrous (*pas de
monstres!*) like the giant masks of carnival. Bloom,
in *Ulysses*, is at first a neat figure in a Dutch
interior, lighting the stove in the early morning,
adjusting his braces and stooping to rub the cat.
With his little routine and typical mental patter
he is our neighbour, the familiar dirty dog or
homme moyen sensuel. But before the book has
gone far, he has become the demigod of an under-

world, a solitary Neptune sitting at the bottom
of his aquarium and staring at the shapes that
loom around him, the fish that suddenly glints and
darts away. . . . In the limbo of the *Childermass*,
Satters and Pulley, pantomime versions of Bouvard and Pécuchet nearing the day of judgment,
meet on an infernal riverfront like old school
chums, grotesquely true to type—Satters is even
wearing football shorts and a tasselled cap as well
as his Mons medal. As they plod on over the
pneumatic cloudway beside the Styx of this
space-time region they become more and more
Protean in shape and character : Gog and Magog :
'good sorts' concealing a multitude of selves,
sinister and comic, each with appropriate mask
and roar; all this behind the old school tie and
club colour. Neither Joyce nor Lewis can keep
the average man for long; a devil dance with
Lamaic headgear begins.

Return from them to the demure puppets of
Flaubert—for Bouvard and Pécuchet are puppets,
over whom, invisibly, their author towers; they
remain in their place, he in his.

The importance for the novel of Flaubert's
discovery that the commonplace itself is epical
can hardly be exaggerated. Human stupidity,
the average, the accustomed gesture, the sentimental thought, the scientific catchword—these
are as eternal as trees and stones. Other writers

and painters have realized this at times in their work, but Flaubert was the first to assert it as a principle. Only an artist who is both great and certain of himself can employ such a method with success: even with Flaubert's guidance, Joyce for example, giving in to the banality of his material, becomes often banal himself, and Lewis, resisting his material, snarls and nags at it.

· · ·

An artistic acceptance of the commonplace— that is supremely difficult.

· · · ·

More difficult now perhaps than in Flaubert's time, because we have a surfeit of banality exaggerated and exploited everywhere. During his eastern travels Flaubert visited the column of Pompey in Alexandria, and found that a certain Thompson, of Sunderland, had carved his name on the base in letters six feet high which could be seen from a quarter of a mile away. Our own streets belong to innumerable Thompsons, whose names are printed all sizes and colours, alongside a picture of a beerbottle or a woman cleaning her teeth; from a train window we see a field of cows ruminating round a terrific placard, on which some Brobdingnagian cow grins over its shoulders and breathes a balloon of printed nonsense; the continental visitor to London is met by the big black-and-white stationboard on the platform— 'London where Abdullas come from'.

· · ·

The invisible god. Paris (early in the morning) :
'Un, deux, trois . . . à droite, à gauche . . . et
enfin . . . Mesdames, messieurs, c'est ici Radio-
Paris'. During Sunday afternoons jazz records,
then a Cockney voice breaks in : 'People, I've got
some *terribly* good news for you. Button's Rubber
Boots are offering you magnificent prizes for the
holidays : hampers, cigars, turkey. . . .' This
drivel is moaned out in several thousand drawing-
rooms, till then the repositories of *objets d'art*,
which could be seen, but did not speak. . . .

. . .

The newspapers. An Englishman arrested in
Russia. Let us pray. News from the Far East :
China is still attacking Japan so that the Japanese
have been obliged to advance south of the great
wall. Does old age exist? The man with the
biggest moustaches in the world has kissed
Amy Johnson. Mr. Hugh Walpole, 'This book
is as original as the solar system'. Armistice Day.
Glorious Goodwood. Guinness is good for you.
Murders and an earthquake. Craven 'A' prevents sore throats. Boulter's Lock. My greatest
friend lies very ill, by James Douglas. Letters
in *The Times*. Gandhi's goat. Society : 'Little
Belvoir is the home of Captain and Mrs. J.
D. Player, who had stipulated that the guests
should appear dressed as children under fourteen.
Rhymes on the wall, nursery pictures and toys
were used to make the ballroom represent a
nursery. Among the guests were Lord Northland,

Mrs. Edward Greenhall, Lord and Lady Brown-
low, Lady Anne Bridgeman, Captain Henry
Broughton,' etc. Lady Oxford visits Drages.
Are you this man, or that? *La belle poitrine.*
Will readers send in poems of their own? The
world of art: 'So-and-so is unique as the
only living English composer who is also an
ex-guards officer.' Amen. Net circulation
300,000,000,000,000,000,000.

.   .   .

The man-in-the-street drinks his beer when it
is watered or poisoned with chemicals, and
calmly digests his newspaper—the banality and
lies of the day, reinforced with a ruthless sub-
humanity.

.   .   .

And the whole fabric of which the press and
'public life' are the facing is breaking up. You
can put your head through the cracks.

.   .   .

This sort of remark was common among young
poets (the *good* ones) a couple of years ago:
'Many of us see in the advertisements of the
Saturday Evening Post the true poetry of America
(the jazz age, the flicks, home comfort, etc.)'.
The remark was fake, but it shows the extent of
discouragement that a poet may feel before the
spectacle of a 'universal cretinism'.

.   .   .

Remember: The old trinity of the poet—God,

man, and nature—has become now the poet, the man-in-the-street, the street.

.   .   .

'Ce que j'écris présentement [*Bovary*] risque d'être du Paul de Kock si je n'y mets une forme profondément littéraire; mais comment faire du dialogue trivial qui soit bien écrit? il le faut pourtant, il le faut.'

'La bêtise est quelque chose d'inébranlable, rien ne l'attaque sans se briser contre elle.'

'Et d'ailleurs le commun, le chétif, le bête, le mesquin, n'ont-ils pas des attractions irrésistibles? Pourquoi tant de maris couchent-ils avec leur cuisinière? Pourquoi la France a-t-elle voulu Louis XVIII après Napoléon?'

Letters of Flaubert.

.   .   .

How to make art from triviality? It is not enough merely to be aware of triviality and to incorporate it. Mr. Day Lewis, one of the best of our young poets, constantly has passages like this:

You 'll be leaving soon and it 's up to you, boys,
Which shall it be? You must make your choice.
There 's a war on, you know. Will you take your stand
In obsolete forts or in no-man's land?

It is symbolic, the flat phrases are there by in-tention, but except that the poet is aware of banality, he gives us no more that is poetry than we got in Squire's rugger matches:

Outside; and a mob hailing cabs, besieging the station,
Sticks, overcoats, scarves, bowler hats, intensified faces,
Rushes, apologies, voices: ' Simpson's at seven,'
'Hallo, Jim,' 'See you next term,' 'I just seen old Peter.'
They go to their homes, to catch trains, all over the city,
All over England; or, many, to make a good night of it,
Eat oysters, drink more than usual, dispute of the match,
For the match is all over, and what, being done, does
    it matter?

What indeed? Squire's is only special reporting.
Mr. Day Lewis is above that, but by using the
same reporter's-jargon he debases the currency of
his verse.

      .   .   .

Flaubert, of course, was not a poet; he took
the prose, or external, view of life which being
detached is more capable of assimilating difficult
material. What the ordinary man does and says
is ordinary; the writer who is going to write about
ordinary people and not about heroes must,
therefore, find a way of overcoming this difficulty;
and Flaubert says that it can only be done by
means of literary form and the style of the author.
In his actual *writing* the novelist must reflect the
grandeur of antiquity, while he assimilates what
is typical and universal in modern life. For
the success of this method see Flaubert's own
writings; for its decadence, the novels and satires
of Anatole France.

      .   .   .

More than this, there is the complex relation
between the novelist and the characters he is
writing about. For his *Bovary* and *Bouvard*

Flaubert deliberately chose characters with whom he had nothing in common. His letters are full of the contradiction that he hates and despises his characters, but that he *is* Bovary, he *is* Bouvard and Pécuchet. The distinction, which he himself never elucidates, is between what he hates in life and what in art. The Bovarys and Bouvards irritate and bore him in life—when he sees them walking down the street, or meets them in the corridor at the opera; once, however, they are part of his art their characteristics are unimportant, his distaste evaporates. No artist, whether he is novelist or lyric poet, can find the material of his art distasteful; except when his art fails.

.   .   .

Flaubert's pessimism, unlike some modern developments of it, never extended to literature. He hated action, but only because action expressed badly thoughts which could be better formulated by art. The modern Flaubertian (Joyce) has begun to distrust art, even his own art. The progression of Joyce from *Dubliners* (Flaubertian naturalism) to the night-town gibberish of *Work in Progress* has been in essence a renunciation of literature, a gradual taking to bed. Midway in the decline, like a mountainous and beautiful cancer which has grown without injury but will end by killing the flesh it lives on, there is *Ulysses*, the masterpiece, strangely isolated, of a minor poet, the flower of illness of our age.

.   .   .

Bloom is the one creation of Joyce's which makes him a great, or nearly great, writer. His other books—stories after Flaubert, verses after Yeats, a play after Ibsen—are talented but unimportant. In the *Portrait of the Artist as a Young Man* he applies the method of *Dubliners* to an autobiography written in the third person (cf. *L'Education Sentimentale*) with more originality and warmth. The prose is at times extremely good, but except in dialogue and the description of spiritual trouble, it is still a *foreign* prose which has not outgrown its derivation. The first twenty-two years of Stephen Daedalus, Irish Graecian and conventional minor poet, are recounted in full, and when we reach the end of the book, there does not seem to be any further richness which Joyce can work from that vein. *Ulysses* begins where the *Portrait* leaves off, and its opening pages confirm one's suspicion—that Joyce is merely applying the illumination of a vastly enlarged style to a hangover of the earlier book. Stephen is now a self-conscious Hamlet, obsessed with the aesthete's grudge against the world, answering the coarseness of his companions 'quietly', mooning, phrasemaking and scoring silently (safe in his art) off the world that surrounds him; invested by Joyce with all the self-pity which his new method, the 'interior monologue', can command. He daydreams naturally in blank verse:

Not theirs these clothes,
This speech, these gestures. Their full slow eyes belied

> The words, the gestures eager and unoffending,
> But knew the rancours massed about them and knew
> Their zeal was vain; vain patience to heap and hoard.
> Time surely would scatter all—a hoard heaped by
> The roadside: plundered and passing on.

It is of course natural that Joyce (Stephen), *who is a minor poet imagining himself to be a great one*, should take the opportunity of working off his undigested verse as prose—the above passage is printed as prose—for we know the innocuous level of his finished verse (*Pomes Penyeach*):

> I heard their young hearts crying
> Leeward above the glancing oar
> And heard the prairie grasses sighing
> *No more, return no more !*
>
> O hearts, O sighing grasses,
> Vainly your loveblown bannerets mourn !
> No more will the wild wind that passes
> Return, no more return.

And if Stephen were the Ulysses of the book instead of being its understrapping Hamlet, Joyce would be doing no more with his new prose than Eliot with his new verse: i.e. once more revealing at work the poet who is inadequate to the task of writing poetry, and who puts all the blame on to these difficult times and not on to himself, thus satisfying his self-pity and gaining for his work a poignancy which it only half deserves.

.   .   .

After fifty pages Bloom comes on the scene, and

the book is transformed. The first sentence
warms: 'Mr. Leopold Bloom ate with relish the
inner organs of beasts and fowls. He liked thick
giblet soup, nutty gizzards, a stuffed roast heart,
liver slices fried with crustcrumbs, fried hen cods'
roes. Most of all he liked grilled mutton kidneys,
which gave to his palate a fine tang of faintly
scented urine. Kidneys were in his mind as he
moved about the kitchen softly, righting her
breakfast things on the humpy tray. Gelid light
and air were in the kitchen, but out of doors
gentle summer morning everywhere. Made him
feel a bit peckish. . . .' And from that point,
Bloom is the centre of focus; he is never actually
described, but we see him moving about during
the day, and in the trickle of his thoughts we
know him, his cronies, his wife and child, the
Dublin streets, the sunset over Howth. The
rumination, commonplace and jouissant, is so
characteristic that we have, brought together for
the first time, the lore of the man-in-the-street.
Joyce has created here a universal character (the
only one in modern fiction) and elaborated a
prose-texture, between daydreaming and a mental
cash-register, which at its best is capable of
bringing into the novel material hitherto un-
dreamt of. In Bloom he escapes completely the
self-infatuation shown by Daedalus and is able to
project a side of himself with detachment, despite
the subjective method. And this is his great
advantage over Proust, for Proust created no
great character except the half-realized, brooding

narrator of the past. Charlus, of course, is not
in the same class as Bloom.

.   .   .

Bloom is the deutero-Joyce, the externalizing
genius without which Joyce would never have
been more than a minor poet. What provoked
him to creation? A general answer will be found
in the drift of these notes, but there was a particular literary stimulus—Flaubert again—which
on internal evidence seems important.

.   .   .

Ulysses describes a day in Dublin in the summer of 1904. In an interesting article[1] Mr. John
Eglinton has described the Joyce of that period—
the long face, with a slight flush suggestive of
dissipation, a straggle of beard, yachting cap,
ashplant, tennis shoes. He expounded excitedly
a theory of æsthetics (*vide* the boring under-
graduate talk in the *Portrait*, and the brilliant
discussion of *Hamlet* in *Ulysses*). Mr. Eglinton adds
that Joyce exactly resembled his hero, Stephen
Daedalus—one was certain of that already. He
cannot place Bloom. Now Bloom was meant
originally for a study in *Dubliners* (1904). Was he
remembered or invented? It is safe to say, from
what we know of Joyce's literary method, that
someone existed who prompted the idea of the
original story; it is possible that the character was
further suggested by some book he had read.
The parallel between the genesis of *Ulysses* and of

[1] *Life and Letters*, December 1932.

Bouvard et Pécuchet is so exact that, taken with Joyce's immense total debt to Flaubert, we might almost assume that Joyce was modelling his book on the lesson of *Bouvard*. Flaubert at first meant his story to be very short, 'a *nouvelle* of about forty pages'; Joyce's intention was the same. Their documentation of material over a long number of years, their distaste (concealing a relish) of the commonplace, their attitude to the bourgeois, and to antiquity: the resemblances are too close to be accidental. Many passages in Flaubert's letters descriptive of his own work apply as much to *Ulysses*. He remarks, for example, that Ulysses is the strongest type in all ancient literature and Hamlet in all modern: these are the two types brought together in *Ulysses*. And this reflection on *Bovary* is even truer of Joyce's novel:

Si le livre que j'écris avec tant de mal arrive à bien, j'aurai établi deux vérités, qui sont pour moi des axiomes, à savoir: d'abord que la poésie est purement subjective, qu'il n'y a pas en littérature de beaux sujets d'art, et qu'Yvetot donc vaut Constantinople; en conséquence l'on peut écrire n'importe quoi aussi bien que quoi que ce soit. L'artiste doit tout élever, il est comme une pompe, il a en lui un grand tuyau qui descend aux entrailles des choses, dans les couches profondes, il aspire et fait jaillir au soleil en gerbes géantes ce qui était plat sous terre et ce qu'on ne voyait pas.

.   .   .

Flaubert's axioms for the poet (novelist) of modern life might be summarized thus:

(1) The splendour of antiquity is set against the stupidity and commonplaceness of the present.

(2) The novelist must not shirk the present.

(3) To render tractable the *ordinariness* of his material he must impose upon it a profoundly literary form.

(4) The splendour of antiquity will still exist in the actual *style* of the novelist, the transformation of what is banal into what is art.

(5) The less one feels anything, the more likely one is to express it as it is in fact—but one must have the capacity to make oneself feel it.

Taken together, these form an æsthetic creed infinitely more deep and subtle than, for example, the attitude of Eliot who solves (1) and (2) by always contrasting present and past as obviously as possible, and who fails adequately to meet the problem stated in (3) and (4). Let us see how far Joyce has followed Flaubert, and what gains and what losses there have been in his divergence.

He would assent without demur to (1) and (2); would agree in principle to (3), but go against it in detail; would dissent from (4) and (5).

The differences between them narrow down to the two questions of *form* and *style*. The *form* of Flaubert's novels is determined finally by some moral or philosophical principle, e.g. Bovarysm or the tragedy of romantic illusion, Bouvardism or the comedy of triumphant stupidity; and the *style* is continuous and detached, always rising superior to its matter, as the author is apart from and above his characters. Flaubert's style invariably contains.

The *form* of *Ulysses* is awkward, lumbering and external, like the exoskeleton of a giant crustacean. Some unity is attained by the limitation of events to Dublin and of time to twenty-four hours; so far, so good. But the Homeric structure of the episodes, each of which corresponds to an episode in the *Odyssey*, the symbolization of parts of the human body, the particular art, symbol and technic which each episode is supposed to represent: these exist only in Joyce's imagination and not in *Ulysses* at all. The various recurring themes, 'Ayenbite of Inwit', Bloom's mourning for his son and the mystical kinship between Bloom and Stephen, which are meant to be central, are completely lost in the welter of narrative.

The *style* of *Ulysses* is faceted and changing, where Flaubert's is dominating and continuous. It is in the use of many styles, the supple opportunism of his prose, that Joyce advances beyond Flaubert. Obviously he sacrifices much, in unity and control, by taking this new step from one style to many; where the characters are boring, the book bores; many passages are unintelligible, neutral, nonsensical because the matter is such and the author does not transmute it. But he gains in the number of effects, in the possibilities of inflection and of transition from one level to another. Flaubert drives his style straight through the landscape like a canal; Joyce's turns with every contour. Mr. Edmund Wilson [1] has said that in *Ulysses* the movements of Naturalism and Symbolism meet for the first time. He exaggerates, perhaps, the effect of Symbolism (this is the theme of his book); but Joyce's *musical* development of language obviously owes much to the Symbolists (who were themselves influenced by music, Wagner's in particular). The Sirens episode in *Ulysses* is narrative raised to a pitch of musical virtuosity such as we find nowhere else in English prose.

. . .

By his greater flexibility of style Joyce has extended Flaubert's conception of the commonplace-comic into *literature* as well as life. The use of parody in *Ulysses*, baffling to the casual reader, is brilliant and original. It varies in its effect from verbal slapstick to pages of pure tranquillized prose. The chapter of parodies, which begins with *Beowulf* and ends in a whirl of polyglot slang, contains passages of astounding beauty. What is perhaps the finest episode in the book—Bloom's reverie on the seashore, where he sits watching the girls on the sands—is written throughout in a style which incorporates the phrases of the *Home Companion* and mingles with the girls' talk: a style which is often commonplace in detail but rises to great beauty of its own. The chapter begins:

The summer evening had begun to fold the world in its mysterious embrace. Far away in the west the sun was

[1] *Axel's Castle*, Scribner's, 1931.

setting and the last glow of all too fleeting day lingered
lovingly on sea and strand, on the proud promontory of
dear old Howth guarding as ever the waters of the bay, on
the weed-grown rocks along Sandymount shore and, last
but not least, on the quiet church whence there streamed
forth at times upon the stillness the voice of prayer to her
who is in her pure radiance a beacon ever to the storm-
tossed heart of man, Mary, star of the sea.

Bloom, the girls, the music and voices coming
from the church, the sunset, the lap of waves, a
crackle of fireworks in the night sky: these are
brought together in modulations of prose which
Joyce has never surpassed. Here, indeed, the
style has the mastery which Flaubert demanded—
though of a very different sort from his. There is
a passage in the *Portrait of the Artist as a Young Man*,
written eight years before *Ulysses*, which throws
light on this development of Joyce's style:

> He drew forth a phrase from his treasure and spoke it
> softly to himself:
> —A day of dappled seaborne clouds.
> The phrase and the day and the scene harmonized in a
> chord. Words. Was it their colour? He allowed them to
> glow and fade, hue after hue; sunrise gold, the russet and
> green of apple orchards, azure of waves, the grey-fringed
> fleece of clouds. No, it was not their colours: it was the
> poise and balance of the period itself. Did he then love the
> rhythmic rise and fall of words better than their associations
> of legend and colour? Or was it that, being as weak of sight
> as he was shy of mind, he drew less pleasure from the
> contemplation of the glowing sensible world through the
> prism of a language many-coloured and richly storied than
> from the contemplation of individual emotions mirrored
> perfectly in a lucid supple periodic prose?

Two phrases there will be found useful in con-
sidering Joyce's literary method. 'The phrase
and the day and the scene harmonized in a

chord'—that is what Joyce is trying all the time
to do: in his recent work he has sacrificed everything, including intelligibility, in order to attain
it. The second phrase in the above passage which
helps further to explain Joyce's intention is the
distinction between two kinds of prose, one
'mirroring perfectly', the other bunching and
refracting objects as in a prism. At the time of
the *Portrait*, Joyce made the Flaubertian choice
of the first; since, he has adopted the other. The
sentences of his mature prose reflect images like a
decanter stopper held up and twirled slowly in
the light.

.   .   .

Twelve points about 'Ulysses'. (1) Joyce discovers
and isolates the present: the 'ineluctable modality'
of the moment.

(2) Joyce is sensible to verbal, as Wagner and
Debussy are to musical sound. His imagination
starts from words and not towards them. There
is a good deal of piano-tuning in *Ulysses*—too
many dead notes. Joyce's method: a verbal
musicalism.

(3) Chief influences: Homer, Rabelais, Shakespeare, Flaubert, Vico.

(4) *Ulysses*, the first gigantic step away from
the novels in ready-mades, the essays in fancy-
dress, the verse in mittens.

(5) The novel-form of the future will probably
be brief: Joyce has said so much that now may
be taken as said: we must expect the next master-

piece to be spare and dynamic, suggesting in a word the processes Joyce has revealed at length.

(6) The novel in English nearest to *Ulysses* is probably, despite huge differences, *Tristram Shandy*. As a literary encyclopaedia, Burton's *Anatomy*.

(7) Articulation of thought, a shaft of light let down into gloom and revealing in its foggy gold the motes stirring.

(8) Joyce's is the conscious use of those quarter-tones and overtones, the meaning echoes which poets have always used unconsciously.

(9) Pain—the Walpurgis Night. Joyce has never been able to detach this from himself; it remains like a crippled limb, the ligaments of which after healing have been left unbroken.

(10) Bloom. Aura of the body; curiosity about the nearest object; poetry of distance (desire).

(11) In Bloom, the comedy of associative thought. At lunch-time he is still unconsciously remembering the funeral he had attended in the morning; as he munches, there is at the bottom of his mind the image of a sleek rat scouting the graveyard. On the counter 'under a sandwich-bell lay, on a bier of bread, one last, one lonely, last sardine of summer.'

(12) Bloom the looker-on, not protagonist (there is none), a new Everyman.

.   .   .

An immense silence pervades *Ulysses*. Behind

the comedy, the clatter of streets, newspaper offices, saloon bars, there is the squat figure, sphinxlike and mysterious, of Bloom, Gog Magog of this hurlyburly, ruminating in his own shade. Never, perhaps, has the final solitude of the individual been more poignantly and forcibly expressed; we feel that nothing can make a window in the walls of the ego of this ordinary man. He is alone. The duologues, the passages of arms or love, of the past have dwindled down to this trickle of thoughts. Round him—the streets like strips of a bad wall-pattern, the pavements like flypaper, a neurasthenic's dream.

GERARD MANLEY HOPKINS

I

In the class-room of the future there will be a
text framed and hung over the head of the master,
'Beware of critics', to which the pupils will
silently point when at the end of an hour's
monologue they find that their master has been
talking, not about Shakespeare, not about Milton
or Shelley, but about himself. And in a higher
form, written in even larger letters, will be
another notice: 'Criticism is the attempt to
substitute taste for genius—the taste of the critic
for the genius of the poet'; and in the light of
that candour the schoolboys of the future will be
allowed to walk their own ways.

An instance of critical bungling is the harm
done to a poet, Gerard Manley Hopkins, even by
critics whose intention has been to recommend
him. Hopkins was born in 1844 and died in
1889. His first critic, Robert Bridges, recognized
Hopkins as a fine poet and proved his admiration
by keeping his poems in cold storage for thirty
years, releasing at last, in 1918, a selection of
Hopkins's poetry, which was enlarged twelve
years later by another editor. He was thus
given a false position from the start. Between
1918 and 1932 these criticisms were made of

Hopkins: (1) that he was the most difficult
English poet, in whom religion stifled art (I. A.
Richards); (2) that he was difficult and at
times incomprehensible, and that wilfulness and
a 'naked encounter between sensualism and
asceticism' spoilt much of his best work (Robert
Bridges); (3) that he was a lyrist, akin to Shelley,
and his 'central point of departure' was the
Ode to a Skylark (J. Middleton Murry); (4) that
Hopkins was on the one hand fundamentally
Miltonic, and on the other fundamentally Shakespearean (various writers; two groups); and
(5) that he was a post-war poet, the leader of a
new school of poets. The last view is popular
with anthologists.

Since the war there have been two discoveries
of importance to poetry: the modern discovery
of Donne, and now the revelation, amazing in
its unexpectedness, of Hopkins. Some difference
of opinion about him is natural, but the jumble
of critical nonsense quoted above might seem
incredible if one had not read it with one's own
eyes. Where did Mr. Murry find his skylark
poet? Hopkins wrote two sonnets on the skylark, neither of which has any connection with
Shelley beyond subject - matter. Two of his
longest poems describe shipwreck: perhaps then
Hopkins is repeating *The Wreck of the Hesperus*?
The argument whether Hopkins is Miltonic or
Shakespearean has more interest because there
are elements in his verse of both: but he was
also influenced by Swinburne and the author of

Beowulf: why not admit that Hopkins is fundamentally himself? The criticisms of Bridges and
of Mr. I. A. Richards are worth answering. But
there are two facts about Hopkins—that he was
a Victorian in style, outlook, and feeling, and
that he was a Catholic priest who wrote poetry
to the glory of God: these facts have been
recognized by no critic whom I can trace.

The most important event in Hopkins's life
was his conversion in 1866, at the age of twenty-
two. Till then he had been, on the surface at
least, another Swinburne, precocious, sensitive,
less diffused, more meticulous, but sowing his
sweet pastoral oats and slipping back through
sunsets and books of Cavalier verse into Greek
mythology. He began by imitating Keats, but
afterwards came to dislike what he called the
unmanly and enervating qualities in Keats's
character, and wrote in a letter to Coventry
Patmore:

> It appears that he said something like 'O for a life of
> impressions rather than thoughts'. . . . His contem-
> poraries, as Wordsworth, Byron, Shelley, and even Leigh
> Hunt, right or wrong, still concerned themselves with
> great causes, as liberty and religion; but he lived in
> mythology and fairyland, the life of a dreamer: neverthe-
> less I feel and see in him the beginnings of something
> opposite to this. . . .

(Is not that the very accent of a Victorian?)
From an early age he had felt and seen 'the
beginnings of something opposite to this' in
himself. At the age of twelve, he described a
schoolfellow in his diary as 'a kaleidoscopic,

parti - coloured, harlequinesque, thaumatropic being'; a note not heard in his poetry till twenty years later. A vein of resistance ran counter to the usual delights of the poet's boyhood, which was otherwise Swinburnian, and found outlet in an occasional prank like fasting from salt or abstention from drinking liquids for a week. His artistic sensibilities, even as a child, were so wide and various that, while he allowed them to develop, his instinct hardened against submission to them.

That brings me to the third fact which has been overlooked: Hopkins was in his sensibility and in the range of his perceptions not only a poet but a musician and a painter. This can be seen plainly enough in his poetry. He was an accomplished musician, fond of composing songs and fugues, and his skill as a painter was sufficient for his biographer [1] to record that 'had his career not been shaped by other incidents he would undoubtedly have adopted painting as a profession'. Some degree of ambidexterity in the arts is perhaps common among poets, particularly minor poets; but in Hopkins we have the case of a great poet who could use his sensibilities as a musician and painter, not merely in the by-practice of these arts, not merely as an enrichment or addition to his poetry, but as an integral part of his poetic genius. There have been plenty

[1] G. F. Lahey, S.J., *Gerard Manley Hopkins*, Oxford Press, 1930. I am indebted to the Oxford Press for permission to quote from their edition of Hopkins's *Poems* and from Lahey's book.

of poets who could imitate or borrow effects from other arts; but few, very few who could employ such means and stimulus *poetically*. The 'difficulty' of his work—which has been grossly exaggerated—lies in the range of his artistic feeling and perception. Once his rhythms and idiom are understood, he presents far less difficulty than, for example, Shakespeare. Here is the painter:

> Crossing the Common, October 13, a fine sunset—great gold field; along the earth-line a train of dark clouds of knopped or clustery make pitching over at the top the way they were going; higher a slanting race of tapered or else coiling fish-like flakes such as are often seen; the gold etched with brighter gold and shaped in sandy places and looped and waved all in waterings. . . .
>
> . . . But what I note it all for is this: before, I had always taken the sunset and the sun as quite out of gauge with each other, as indeed physically they are, for the eye after looking at the sun is blunted to everything else and if you look at the rest of the sunset you must cover the sun, but to-day I inscaped them together and made the sun the true eye and ace of the whole, as it is. It was all active and tossing out light and started as strongly forward from the field as a long stone or a boss in the knob of the chalice-stem: it is indeed by stalling it so, that it falls into scape with the sky.

His poems are crowded with landscapes. No other English poet has worked so intensely on such a ground of realistic perceptions, the exact yet ecstatic perceptions of a poet alone not merely in the presence of Nature, but of Nature circled by the glory of God. Here is a bit of pure landscape painting, an oil in the gallery of poets' water-colours:

Nothing is so beautiful as spring—
  When weeds, in wheels, shoot long and lovely and lush;
  Thrush's eggs look little low heavens, and thrush
Through the echoing timber does so rinse and wring
The ear, it strikes like lightnings to hear him sing;
  The glassy peartree leaves and blooms, they brush
  The descending blue; that blue is all in a rush
With richness; the racing lambs too have fair their fling.

What is all this juice and all this joy?
  A strain of the earth's sweet being in the beginning
In Eden garden.—Have, get, before it cloy,
  Before it cloud, Christ, Lord, and sour with sinning,
Innocent mind and Mayday in girl and boy.
  Most, O maid's child, thy choice and worthy the winning.
                                        (1877.)

In *Spelt from Sibyl's Leaves*, though he still begins
by expressing landscape, you have the musician:

Earnest, earthless, equal, attunable, | vaulty, voluminous
    . . . stupendous
Evening stráins to be tíme's vást, | womb-of-all, home-of-all,
    hearse-of-all night.
Her fond yellow hornlight wound to the west, | her wild
    hollow hoarlight hung to the height
Waste: her earliest stars, earl-stars, | stárs principal, over-
    bend us,
Fíre-féaturing heaven. For earth | her being has unbound,
    her dapple is at an end, as-
tray or aswarm, all throughther, in throngs; | self ín self
    steepèd and páshed—qúite
Disremembering, dísmémbering | áll now. Heart, you
    round me right
With: Oúr évening is over us; oúr night | whélms, whélms,
    ánd will end us.
Only the beak-leaved boughs dragonish | damask the tool-
    smooth bleak light; black,
Ever so black on it. Oúr tale, O oúr oracle! | Lét life,
    wáned, ah lét life wind
Off hér once skeíned stained veíned varíety | upon, áll on
    twó spools; párt, pen, páck
Now her áll in twó flocks, twó folds—black, white; | right,
    wrong; reckon but, reck but, mind

But thése two; wáre of a wórld where bút these | twó tell,
    each off the óther; of a rack
Where self-wrung, self-strung, sheathe- and shelterless, |
    thóughts agaínst thoughts ín groans grínd.

                 (1881.)

That is Hopkins's music at its most magnificent
and intricate. Note in line three the use of
musical device to convey the moon's yellow and
the frosty other parts of the sky: the major key
in the first half of the line, and the minor in the
second: the subtle correspondence and variation
of sounds and rhythms from first to second half,
giving the final syncopation of 'waste' which
begins a new line, whereas the original 'west'
ends its half. A similar variation and syncopation
are seen in line ten. 'Let life, waned, ah let life
wind': here the syncopation is one of thought
and even syntax; it would cease, for example,
if we were to substitute an infinitive verb for the
past participle 'waned'—'Let life wend, ah let
life wind', apart from its flatness, has lost the
essential syncopation of Hopkins's phrase.

Mr. Arthur Waley, describing the verse texture
of the Nō plays of Japan, has remarked that 'the
English poet who comes nearest to doing this
sort of thing is Gerard Manley Hopkins'. He
does not give examples, but from his description
of 'a particular sort of play on words, in which
one word is made to act as a "pivot", functioning
twice over, in different senses', it is possible to
infer the practice of Hopkins he has in mind.
To take an elementary instance, the line:

     Whether at once, as once at a crash Paul . . .

contains the repetition of 'once' with different meanings, and 'at once' becomes in variation 'once at'. Or, more complexly:

> I caught this morning morning's minion, kingdom of daylight's dauphin, dapple-dawn-drawn Falcon in his riding.

And the supreme example:

> Nay in all that toil, that coil, since (seems) I kissed the rod,
> Hand rather, my heart, lo! lapped strength, stole joy,
>   would laugh, chéer.
> Cheer whom though? the hero whose heaven-handling
>   flung me, fóot tród
> Me? or me that fought him? O which one? is it each one?
>   That night, that year
> Of now done darkness I wretch lay wrestling with (my
>   God!) my God.

The use of pivot words here is, I take it, somewhat akin to the texture of the verse in Nō plays.

Yet these devices, analogous to music, are, as Hopkins uses them, intrinsically poetical.

There are countless smaller examples in the poems of his middle period:

> 'Some find me a sword; some
>   The flange and the rail; flame,
> Fang, or flood' goes Death on drum,
>   And storms bugle his fame.
> But wé dream we are rooted in earth—Dust!
> Flesh falls within sight of us, we, though our flower the same,
>   Wave with the meadow, forget that there must
> The sour scythe cringe, and the blear share come.
>   (1876.)

It is even in the transference of accent on a word:

> Both sing sometímes the sweetest, sweetest spells
> Yet both droop deadly sómetimes in their cells.

And it is in single lines:

And frightful a nightfall folded rueful a day . . .

Stigma, signal, cinquefoil token . . .

The cross to her she calls Christ to her, christens her wild
worst best.

I have given examples of the polyphony, so
rich, varied, and ringing, of his grandest work;
there are two strains in his poetry; the other is
the simple melody of Marvell and Vaughan.
He began with it (1866):

> Lilies I show you, lilies none,
> None in Cæsar's gardens blow,—
> And a quince in hand,—not one
> Is set upon your boughs below.

But it was continued later, after the terrific
interruption of the *Wreck of the Deutschland* (1876),
with exquisite effect mingling its tune with the
more loaded polyphonic style; and sometimes
he returned to it for the whole length of a poem.

One other essential of Hopkins's poetry remains
to be mentioned, the vision (foreshadowed in his
schoolboy phrase) of the world as 'dappled,
parti-coloured'. This texture, the artist's sense
of life-texture as he works in his medium, is seen
most strongly in poems like 'Glory be to God for
dappled things', of which it is the theme, but it
is present everywhere in his later work, in the
verbal texture of the poetry.

II

In the preface to his poems Hopkins distinguishes two kinds of rhythm: Running Rhythm (which includes all the common English metres), and Sprung Rhythm, a metrical development peculiarly his own.

'Sprung rhythm,' he says, 'as used in this book, is measured by feet of from one to four syllables, regularly, and for particular effects any number of weak or slack syllables may be used. It has one stress, which falls on the only syllable, if there is only one, or, if there are more, then scanning as above, on the first, and so gives rise to four sorts of feet, a monosyllable and the so-called accentual Trochee, Dactyl, and the First Paeon'. He adds that there are, then, four corresponding natural rhythms; which may be mixed; and it is in the use of a mixed sprung rhythm that he gets his finest and most original effects. The line can be so contracted or expanded that it will emphasize or hover in a way hitherto unknown in English poetry. So we find in the sonnet *Spelt from Sibyl's Leaves* (quoted on page 48) that the line keeps its essential character, though the rhythm is always changing. The first three lines, in which there are many slack syllables, rise and echo with tremendous effect. Line eight has a stabbing beat and emphasis which could result in no other kind of metre:

With: Oúr évening is over us; oúr night | whélms, whélms, ánd will end us.

The two adjacent beats in the first half of the line, followed by three adjacent beats in the second half, achieve an emphasis which might be compared with the trochaic effect of Lear's

Never, never, never, never, never.

Hopkins's line, though more complex, gains a similar effect by its unexpected yet natural rhythm. Here we have indeed a poetry, apparently complicated to the reader unused to it, which follows closely the rhythms of ordinary speech and opens out the English verse line as no other poet has done since Shakespeare.

III

Lahey's book, already mentioned, is memoir rather than biography. Such knowledge as we have of Hopkins's life is contained there. Unfortunately this is very little, and we are given few of the letters written by Hopkins to his friends, though we are allowed to see him in reflection as his friends address him. The atmosphere is scholarly, quiet, sheltered, with that tone of integrity and friendship which we find so often in the letters of Victorians. The intellectual movements of the time make a current in which all these figures bend, yielding perhaps a little stiffly. In their correspondence the gravity of tone, the accent of the schools, the hint of cloister and common - room, and beyond, the pastoral landscape, background of an ordered feeling and worship, and demesne of the poet, are foreign to us who have no experience of such an existence. Victorianism with its high seriousness and endeavour, and its sense of a central importance, seems provincial when it leaves the world of ideas for the world of art. While Hopkins was experiencing his spiritual conversion in the set forms of Oxford, Van Gogh was beginning a battle which is by comparison terrific.

Hopkins was on friendly but not intimate terms with a number of people. The correspondence with Patmore shows him as a man not easily approachable who impressed others by his intellect and vivid integrity. The friendship between these two (Patmore was getting old, though he had not yet written the *Odes*) was perhaps typical. They met only twice, but corresponded regularly for six years. Poetry, religion, a circle of friends—they had much in common; and Patmore wrote to Bridges, after one meeting with Hopkins, that he had 'seldom felt so much attracted towards any man'. He gave in to Hopkins on all critical points affecting his own writing; the *Sponsa Dei* was destroyed as the result of a chance word by the younger man; but though he read eagerly the poems which Hopkins sent him from time to time he could make little of them—for him they were 'veins of pure gold imbedded in masses of impracticable quartz'. Bridges's admiration was hardly more understanding. The other friends to whom he showed his poetry were scholars and minor poets of the type of Digby Dolben and Canon Dixon. Small wonder that if he was going to write great poetry he must escape their atmosphere. This isolation was ensured by the routine of priesthood.

IV

Hopkins is a poet-mystic. His life was divided between religion, poetry, and the contemplation of nature. The search for God took him to nature, rather than human nature. Where Patmore, also a Catholic and a mystic, found in the union of lovers the mystical communion of God and the soul, Hopkins found it in prayer, and in the communion of the soul and nature. His association with his fellow human beings, as it is shown in his poetry, is limited to the contacts of his work as priest and schooolmaster, visits to friends, the sight of strangers living in a warmer world than his own. In nature, and in the torments of spiritual struggle, he came nearest to God. The landscape expressed for him God's presence: *inscape* or *instress* (words he is fond of using) is not merely the artist's apprehension of vital form, but of divine shape. Wherever he can find *inscape*—in the eternal yet ever-changing forms of tree, river, and cloud—he finds God.

What I am in the habit of calling *inscape* is what I above all aim at in poetry.

All the world is full of inscape and chance left free to act falls into an order as well as purpose.

He observed the forms of nature with an amazing attention, and recorded what for him was essential in the most exact detail. His diaries are full of notes such as these:

First fine; then on the road a thunderstorm with hard rain, the thunder musical and like gongs and rolling in great floors of sound.

We drove to St. Rémy. As we approached it the hills 'fledged' with larches which hung in them shaft after shaft like green-feathered arrows.

Noticed also the cornfields below us laid by the rain in curls like a lion's mane very impressive.

.   .   .   .   .

In the train I was noticing that strange rotten-wovey cloud which shapes in leaf over leaf of wavy or eyebrow texture: it is like fine webs or gossamer held down by many invisible threads on the undersides against a wind which between these points kept blowing them into balls. The curious rottenness about them reminds one of that dark green silken oozy seaweed with holes in it which lines and hangs from piers and slubbered wood in the sea.

.   .   .   .   .

Through Paris to Dieppe and by Newhaven home. Day—bright. Sea calm, with little walking wavelets edged with fine eyebrow crispings, and later nothing but a matting or chain-work on the surface, and even that went, so that the smoothness was marbly and perfect, and, between the just-corded near-sides of the waves, rising like fishes' backs and breaking with darker blue the pale blue of the general field; in the very sleek hollows, came out golden crumbs of reflections from the chalk cliffs. Peach-coloured sundown and above some simple gilded masses of cloud, which later became finer, smaller, and scattering away.

.   .   .   .   .

I saw the phenomenon of the sheep flock on the downs again from Croham Hurst. It ran like water-packets on a leaf—that collectively, but a number of globules so filmed over that they would not flush together is the exacter comparison: at a gap in the hedge they were huddled and shaking open as they passed outwards they behaved as the drops would do (or a handful of shot) in reaching the brow of a rising and running over.

.   .   .   .   .

(Lambs.)   They toss and toss; it is as if it were the earth that flung them, not themselves.   It is the pitch of graceful agility.

These jottings were made in 1868, when Hopkins was still writing conventional if exquisite pastoral verse (*Heaven—Haven*); that is, eight years *before* such exact observation became part of his poetry.   The search for inscape is always his object; here he identifies it with the search for God:

I do not think I have ever seen anything more beautiful than the bluebell I have been looking at.   I know the beauty of Our Lord by it.   Its inscape is mixed of strength and grace, like an ash-tree.   The head is strongly drawn over backwards and arched down like a cutwater drawing itself back from the line of the keel.   The lines of the bell strike and overlie this, rayed but not symmetrically, some lie parallel.   They look steely against the paper, the shades lying between the bells and behind the cockled petal-ends and nursing up the precision of their distinctness, the petal-ends themselves being delicately lit.   Then there is the straightness of the trumpets in the bells softened by the slight entasis and by the square splay of the mouth.   One bell, the lowest, some way detached and carried on a longer footstalk, touched out with the lips of the petal.

So intimate is the connection in the poet's mind between God and the shapes of Nature, that his religion makes a distinction in natural objects of those which figure the power and terror of God, and those that are intervening and merciful as Mary.

The two strains in his poetry which I have already mentioned—the mature polyphony, and the earlier simple melody—are employed to express these two conceptions of the appearance of the Divine. The *Wreck of the Deutschland*, his first great poem, in which he attains maturity, is vast and polyphonic, to meet its subject—the praise of God who yet admits pain and destruction in the world. The occasion is a shipwreck in which five nuns were drowned, and I quote a passage which is narrative, and not hymn or argument of faith; these lines reflect and reverberate the faith and 'terror of God' with which the poem begins:

12

On Saturday sailed from Bremen,
    American-outward-bound,
  Take settler and seamen, tell men with women,
    Two hundred souls in the round—
O Father, not under thy feathers nor ever as guessing
The goal was a shoal, of a fourth the doom to be
    drowned;
    Yet did the dark side of the bay of thy blessing
Not vault them, the millions of rounds of thy mercy not
    reeve even them in?

13

Into the snows she sweeps,
    Hurling the haven behind,
  The Deutschland, on Sunday; and so the sky keeps,
    For the infinite air is unkind,
And the sea flint-flake, black-backed in the regular
    blow,
Sitting Eastnortheast, in cursed quarter, the wind;
    Wiry and white-fiery and whirlwind-swivellèd snow
Spins to the widow-making unchilding unfathering deeps.

14

She drove in the dark to leeward,
She struck—not a reef or a rock
But the combs of a smother of sand: night drew her
Dead to the Kentish Knock;
And she beat the bank down with her bows and the
ride of her keel:
The breakers rolled on her beam with ruinous shock;
And canvas and compass, the whorl and the wheel
Idle for ever to waft her or wind her with, these she endured.

15

Hope had grown grey hairs,
Hope had mourning on,
Trenched with tears, carved with cares,
Hope was twelve hours gone;
And frightful a nightfall folded rueful a day
Nor rescue, only rocket and lightship, shone,
And lives at last were washing away:
To the shrouds they took,—they shook in the hurling and
horrible airs.

16

One stirred from the rigging to save
The wild woman-kind below,
With a rope's end round the man, handy and brave—
He was pitched to his death at a blow,
For all his dreadnought breast and braids of thew:
They could tell him for hours, dandled the to and fro
Through the cobbled foam-fleece, what could he do
With the burl of the fountains of air, buck and the flood of
the wave?

17

They fought with God's cold—
And they could not and fell to the deck
(Crushed them) or water (and drowned them) or rolled
With the sea-romp over the wreck.
Night roared, with the heart-break hearing a heart-
broke rabble,
The woman's wailing, the crying of child without
check—
Till a lioness arose breasting the babble,
A prophetess towered in the tumult, a virginal tongue told.

18

Ah, touched in your bower of bone
Are you! turned for an exquisite smart,
Have you! make words break from me here all alone,
Do you!—mother of being in me, heart.
O unteachably after evil, but uttering truth.
Why, tears! is it? tears; such a melting, a madrigal
start!
Never-eldering revel and river of youth,
What can it be, this glee? the good you have there of your
own?

That last stanza, where he breaks off to accuse himself, is one of the finest in all Hopkins: the personal voice speaking, as in great art it occasionally will, without breaking the creation.

For the other strain, plain melody expressing the gentleness of nature and Mary's intervention, there is this passage from *The Blessed Virgin compared to the Air we Breathe*:

Again, look overhead
How air is azurèd;
O how! nay do but stand
Where you can lift your hand
Skywards: rich, rich it laps
Round the four fingergaps.
Yet such a sapphire-shot,
Charged, steepèd sky will not
Stain light. Yea, mark you this:
It does no prejudice.
The glass-blue days are those
When every colour glows,
Each shape and shadow shows.
Blue be it: this blue heaven
The seven or seven times seven
Hued sunbeam will transmit
Perfect, nor alter it.
Or if there does some soft,
On things aloof, aloft,
Bloom breathe, that one breath more
Earth is the fairer for.

Whereas did air not make
This bath of blue and slake
His fire, the sun would shake,
A blear and blinding ball
With blackness bound, and all
The thick stars round him roll
Flashing like flecks of coal,
Quartz-fret, or sparks of salt,
In grimy vasty vault.
  So God was god of old:
A mother came to mould
Those limbs like ours which are
What must make our daystar
Much dearer to mankind;
Whose glory bare would blind
Or less would win man's mind.
Through her we may see him
Made sweeter, not made dim,
And her hand leaves his light
Sifted to suit our sight. . . .

Nowhere else is his melody so perfect.

So this is the dapple of his vision, the division of his poetry, the couple-colour which entranced him in nature—God's grandeur, Mary's comfort.

v

Where he could he praised; but the agony of his spiritual life, the striving to expel doubt is pierced forever by the knowledge that God does not respond. It is worth noting that despite the fact that Jesuit theologians are Thomistic, Hopkins when he became a Jesuit chose to be a disciple of Duns Scotus, whose doctrine admits the element of doubt. His ecstatic perception of nature is always a hymn of praise (*God's Grandeur*, *Spring*, etc.). But nature mirrors doubt also

(*Spelt from Sibyl's Leaves*).   In the end, after the tremendous sonnets of spiritual torment (Nos. 40, 41, 44, 45, 46, 47), the contrast between nature's happiness and his own misery agonizes him; all the beauty he has found in nature emphasizes now his solitude (No. 50):

> Thou art indeed just, Lord, if I contend
> With thee; but, Sir, so what I plead is just.
> Why do sinners' ways prosper? and why must
> Disappointment all I endeavour end?
>   Wert thou my enemy, O thou my friend,
> How wouldst thou worse, I wonder, than thou dost
> Defeat, thwart me?   Oh, the sots and thralls of lust
> Do in spare hours more thrive than I that spend,
> Sir, life upon thy cause.   See, banks and brakes
> Now, leavèd how thick! lacèd they are again
> With fretty chervil, look, and fresh wind shakes
> Them—but not I build; no, but strain,
> Time's eunuch, and not breed one work that wakes.
> Mine, O thou lord of life, send my roots rain.

VI

I have been careful to insist on the importance of one event in this poet's life: his conversion in the year 1866.   That date divides boyhood from maturity and early poems from great poems. Religion hardened him morally and intellectually, provided him with a background infinitely better suited to his genius than Greek myth, and brought into his poetry the polyphony of style, parti-colour of pattern, and expanding, realistic, and passionate force of his great work.   In the face of this it seems to me absurd to speak of damage done to him by conflicts of art and religion, sensuousness and asceticism. The interaction of these forces produced much of his best poetry. A friend wrote of him: 'His mind was too delicate a texture to grapple with the rough elements of life'; and this is true. But it is true also that no other poet has so grappled reality into his imagination, mixing earth with his words. He employed native words, root-words of old stock, rhythms of speech, and compelled them, as did Hardy, by the sheer poetic force and integrity of his mind; but while with Hardy the words remain sometimes awkward, local, or antique, like tough old bits of furniture, in Hopkins they are knocked together, swept along in the one rush of his passion. 'Take breath,' he said, 'and read.' The advice is worth a lot of criticism.

SWINBURNE

Two things stand in the way of modern apprecia-
tion of Swinburne: the legend of the 'poet', and
the bulk of his writings. There is so much of
them, so little of him. He can be crammed into
a phrase, 'the wonderful child', or, maliciously,
'the pseudo-Shelley'; and one eagerly accepts
the portrait of a cockatoo, or a sleep-walker
miraculously crossing the streets and eating
lunches of asparagus in a Holborn restaurant.
They are not complete portraits; but they have
that touch of incongruous human nature which
makes them acceptable. Swinburne is at once
too easy and too difficult for the biographer: even
Gosse, who was a personal friend, succeeded only
in sketching him. It is hardly enough to know
that he had small feet and fluttered his hands,
that at Putney he drank a bottle of beer a day and
pinched babies' cheeks, that he could recite a
whole play of Æschylus from memory (though
this tells us something). One cannot help feeling
that all his friends and visitors who wrote about
him must have missed something—something
essential—until suddenly it is plain that Swinburne was actually like their descriptions (which
concur remarkably), that in fact he was a windy
spirit somehow bundled together with human
characteristics, most of which seem irrelevant.

64

The chief thing about Swinburne, from the point of view of the critic, is that to him poetry was all-important; his life outside his poetry and the reactions from it was negligible. He had one love-affair, which terminated abruptly; much of his life was solitary, and when his health broke he submitted himself to Watts-Dunton, for a period of twenty-eight years, without question. Gosse records that Swinburne explained to him once 'that he did not regard current novels as literature but as life, and that in his absolutely detached existence they took the place of real adventures'. Swinburne's chief reading was Dickens, whose novels he re-read every three years! And his love of Italy and the sea was hardly, in this sense, more realistic. It is as though his physical sensibility exaggerated contact with the outside world a hundred times, so that a footfall became a deafening roar. His whole life, which to us seems like the retirement up a sheltered valley, must in fact have been as shrill and shattering as a journey in the 'tube'. The confusion of his poetry—a sort of Albert Hall echo—comes not from the jarring of unrelated experiences and sensations, but from their universal muffled roar. Just as a camera with the lens sufficiently out of focus will reduce everything on the ground-screen to a similar blur of colours, so Swinburne's imagination worked with the same distorting influence on whatever came into its view. It was a question with him of seeing red, or not seeing at all.

Again and again he uses the same symbols to
describe things as different as a landscape and kiss:

> Forth, ballad, and take roses in both arms,
>   Even till the top rose touch thee in the throat
> Where the least thornprick harms;
> And girdled in thy golden singing-coat,
>   Come thou before my lady and say this . . .

He addresses his ballad exactly as he would his
lady. The raptures of his early poems, profuse
and astonishing as they are, glut the appetite.
What a relief it is in the poem 'At a Month's
End', after the ghost of the seashore and the
night's remembrance and 'love's love forsaken',
to come upon these lines:

> Across, aslant, a scudding sea-mew
>   Swam, dipped, and dropped, and grazed the sea . . .

But again the verse ends:

> . . . And one with me I could not dream you:
>   And one with you I could not be.

Which is matched by twenty other such verses
in the poem. Yet by the same methods he
achieved many of his finest images; the evocation
of the Republican flag, for example, in the
'Epilogue' to *Songs Before Sunrise*:

> For if the swimmer's eastward eye
> Must see no sunrise—must put by
> The hope that lifted him and led
> Once, to have light about his head,
>   To see beneath the clear low sky
> The green foam-whitened wave wax red
>   And all the morning's banner fly—
> Then as earth's helpless hopes go down,
> Let earth's self in the dark tides drown.

Only Swinburne could have written that.

His love of freedom and humanity is obviously sincere, and productive of much of his best work. What then of the sadism and exuberant sensuality of the first *Poems and Ballads*? Their roots were largely in his imagination. The references in a letter to Lord Houghton about his 'infamous' *Dolores* are cynical, delightedly so. About a novel, *Lesbia Brandon*, he wrote in 1867: 'I flatter myself it will be more offensive and objectionable to Britannia than anything I have yet done'. This is bravado, and yet with most writers it would hint insincerity. *Dolores*, after all, was then his most famous poem, and Edmund Gosse, in a little known essay published in 1875, describes it as a unique and magnificent achievement of Swinburne's genius. That was the general opinion of the time, and Swinburne probably shared it. Then there are his far-fetched and elaborate hatreds: Hazlitt's name must never be mentioned because of his attacks on Coleridge; an edition of Shakespeare is violently attacked in a long review because its editor is Hazlitt's grandson. Much of his critical prose is spoilt by irrelevant abuse and sheer bad writing, which never occurred in his worst poems. The seventeen sonnets collected under the title *Dirae* were no doubt in many cases remotely and unhistorically felt, but the feeling is there, with terrific force, and one does not question their genuineness. So long as he caught fire, his sincerity is unquestionable; and even the productions of those last twenty years at Putney, though the genius

is gone, are never mere empty exercise or in-
genuity. He was always, completely, a poet,
even when he was a bad one—that perhaps is the
most that can be said. Imperfect as even his
best work is, it is in this sense pure art, and not
like Wagner's the result of an imperfectly achieved
artistic sincerity. It is the fact that he never
ceased to be and think as a poet which is finally
responsible for his excesses. He did not, like
Shelley, leave countless poems unwritten; on the
contrary, he very often went on writing long after
he should have stopped. A lyric like the one
which begins:

> If love were what the rose is,
>   And I were like the leaf

is weakened by long antithesis and repetition.
There is almost no poem of his that can be called
faultless, in spite of the claims of various admirers.
One reader will exalt *Erechtheus*, which perhaps
rightly has been called the most Greek of any
English poem. Another prefers *Tristram in
Lyonesse*. I cannot agree that either of these
long poems is perfect: something is lacking in
both, particularly in *Tristram in Lyonesse*, despite
its superb prelude and passages of description
and conversation between the lovers, which are
as fine as anything Swinburne ever wrote. *Siena*
is for me a more complete and organic poem than
either of these.

Any discussion of Swinburne is bound to
mention his literary influences. What a mass

of them there is! Hugo, Baudelaire, Shelley, Æschylus, Wagner, Landor, the border ballads, Villon, Catullus, Aristophanes, the Elizabethan dramatists — to name only a few! And the astonishing thing is that all these influences were particular and vital. Very few of Swinburne's poems can be called derivative, and only perhaps in the case of Landor and Baudelaire can it be definitely said that the effect was bad. Hardly a poem that is not characteristic of Swinburne himself, whatever its origin. His metrical skill, particularly in the management of long irregular rhythms, as in *Super Flumina Babylonis* and *Hertha*, is unequalled in subtlety and variety; but it is of course a mistake to pretend that the sound is everything and the meaning nowhere. The technique of his later work at least equals the earlier.

It is the bulk of verses, neither good nor bad but typical, which makes a formidable bar to one's enjoyment of Swinburne. The particular boredom of reading too much Swinburne is that of a long train journey offering too many views. But his best is fine and unmistakable, and there is more of it than most readers imagine.

D. H. LAWRENCE

LAWRENCE has been compared with Carlyle, with
Rousseau, and even with Jesus: with Carlyle as
prose rhapsodist and minor prophet; with Rousseau because he sought a return to nature and
the creation of a new 'natural man'. Mr.
Richard Aldington, in one of the best personal
essays on Lawrence, describes him as 'a Nietzsche
who effected a transvaluation not of intellectual
values, but of fundamental human values'. That
suggests more closely the sort of influence other
comparisons are hinting at. The emphasis, it
will be noticed, is on Lawrence as man and
prophet rather than artist, for essentially, he has
little in common with either Rousseau or Carlyle,
Jesus or Nietzsche. But he is a personal figure of
the Romantic kind among contemporaries who are
self-effacing in their art, and he has a 'message'.

The importance of that message has been over-
stressed: detached from his art, it is neither very
deep nor very original, and what is new in it is
often extreme and even silly. I do not believe
that he effected, or is likely in the future to effect,
any 'transvaluation of fundamental human
values'; his influence will probably be felt

chiefly as a corrective to its opposite in literature
—the cerebral poet of the type of Eliot. 'It takes
application', Mr. Eliot has written, 'and a kind
of genius to believe anything, and to believe
anything (I do not mean merely to believe in some
"religion") will probably become more and more
difficult as time goes on. . . . We await, in
fact . . . the great genius who shall triumphantly
succeed in believing *something*.' Well, Lawrence,
alone among his contemporaries, achieved this
difficult feat of believing in something, and
though he wavered in that belief the more he
asserted it, he has had a following. His message
was perhaps the only personal one to which the
post-war generation could turn for hope or
understanding of itself. I emphasize the fact
that it was personal; because the usual messages
of to-day are political, and have been so from the
early days of Shaw and Wells to the Five-Year-
Plan crusades of Soviet Russia. The only
alternative ideal to Communism at the moment
is some form of religion which is individual
rather than political. The *Wandervögel*, bands
of hikers, sunbathers, and sex-primitives, are
manifestations of the crude attempt at a new
orientation of life-values—crude, because indi-
vidualism is aimed at by means of mass-move-
ments. Lawrence provided a solution (whatever its faults) which keeps the integrity of the
individual. For this side of his writings—the
prophetic and moralistic, which finally dominated
his art—I suggest the comparison, not with

Rousseau or Nietzsche, but with a lesser writer, V. V. Rozanov.

Rozanov, like Lawrence, was an authentic rebel. His books were written before the war, towards the end of the bourgeois regime, in which he made a final attempt to assert the violence of individual feeling, and he had the sort of reputation in Russia that Lawrence is enjoying at the moment here—one critic (Prince Mirsky, I think) described him as the greatest Russian writer after Tolstoy and Dostoevsky. Like Lawrence, he was compared with Rousseau. *Solitaria* and *Fallen Leaves*, the two books of his which have been translated into English, are the prose equivalents of *Pansies*, and they express a belief and intuition similar in many ways to Lawrence's. If we allow for the fact that Rozanov is intensely Russian and Lawrence intensely English, many passages are interchangeable. 'Paganism is morning; Christianity, evening.' 'Christianity must become phallic'—these aphorisms from *Fallen Leaves* might as easily have come from *Apocalypse*, *Fantasia of the Unconscious*, or a discussion in almost any of Lawrence's novels. 'I never think,' exclaimed Rozanov, 'I only laugh and cry.' Sex was the electricity of his world ('sex *is* power'), as of Lawrence's, and he preached the validity of the instincts and their healing power for the over-civilized man. His attack on a complacent bourgeois society was directed equally against the forms of literature which that society had absorbed and falsified by making 'acceptable'. It is the fundamental protest of the artist who turns from literature to life, who asserts the supremacy of his own personality. Rozanov claimed that there was more genuine literature in his washing-books than in Turgenev's *Letters to Madame Viardo*. His washing-books have not survived, but it would be a mistake to miss his paradox with the obvious retort.

> Not literature [he writes], but literariness is terrible, literariness of the soul, literariness of life. . . .
> A writer must suppress the writer in himself ('authorship', literariness). . . .
> I believe the essence of literature is a false one; not that 'the present time' and 'those writers' are wrong; but all that domain is wrong, and in its every being, through the seeds from which it sprang:
> 'Now I am going *to write* and *let them all read*.'
> Why 'I' and why should they read?

Here and elsewhere (the contradictions don't matter) Rozanov does express a fundamental truth about literature which writers have come more and more to feel—the falseness of the speaking mask, betrayal of the essential silence behind. In bringing to consciousness the unconscious life, and in preaching submission to the instincts (how else, except by an act of will?), Lawrence was faced with the same innate contradiction. For whom, too, was he writing?—not for those who were nearest to the condition of living he desired: and the readers who would understand him best were at the opposite pole of sophistication—how could they achieve more than a play-acting of his principles? That was the difficulty —which Lawrence perhaps half felt. At his best,

he turned to life (the life in himself) instinctively;
Rozanov did so ostentatiously.

There are, of course, important differences
between them. Lawrence is far more of an artist.
Rozanov, with his wild furious little paragraphs,
which thunder and crackle like an electric train
going over points, seems always as though he is
wanting to provide the material for a masterpiece and to leave it unwritten—which in fact
is what he succeeded in doing. (Much of Lawrence, in the same way, is 'unwritten'.) But
though he sometimes resorts to mystification, and
leaves the reader to rummage in his literary
dustbin, he is by no means negligible. It is
noticeable that when he goes to extremes, it is to
show a flash of insight, whereas Lawrence at his
most extreme is usually most silly. His ideas cut
deeper than Lawrence's, partly because they are
realistic, but also because he understood the
peculiarity of his position as Lawrence never did.

Before finishing with comparisons, there is
another worth mentioning, and as it is concerned
with Lawrence's art, it comes nearer the quick.
A number of critics have argued that Lawrence
is the counterpart in literature of Van Gogh.
Their juxtaposition seems tempting. Both began
by depicting the life of mining villages, 'mixing
earth with their paints' (Van Gogh did this in
fact); both were driven south by illness and by
desire of the sun, which gave them fuller life,
the brilliance of colour and flaming symbol they
missed in the north. Van Gogh went mad after

a life of hardship and killed himself; Lawrence died of consumption—both before they reached middle age. As men, however, they were of very different character; there was a good deal of the feminine in Lawrence, in his permeating sense of sex, his love of touch and distrust of the intellect, his restlessness and instability; among friends and in his marriage, even, Lawrence was always lonely, while Van Gogh, though capable of far deeper love, became a solitary; Lawrence was a mystic, Van Gogh a saint—the opposition could be prolonged. In their art, again, there is resemblance up to a point: both succeeded, as no artist had done before them, in bringing the still-life to life; landscapes, trees, flowers ran with a new sap in their work. But the vision and sensibility of each was utterly different. Van Gogh's is hard, flaming, tortured, passionate, and felt with the hand and eye of a workman in his surroundings. Lawrence's is softer, ecstatic, interfused and queered with nostalgia—the longing, rather than the grip, is felt. A comparison of the two, though useful, must always be detrimental to Lawrence. Note their letters, the strength of the one, the weakness of the other. They are worlds apart.

'I see Van Gogh so sadly,' Lawrence wrote to one of his correspondents. 'If he could only have set the angel of himself clear in relation to the animal of himself, clear and distinct but always truly related, in harmony and union, he need not have cut off his ear and gone mad.'

What Lawrence objected to in the mad geniuses of the end of the century—Van Gogh, Dostoevsky, Strindberg—was ostensibly a destructiveness or 'death-urge' in their views of life: what really appalled him, a sick man preaching health, was the hardness and gripping vitality of their art. His own substitute for madness being hysteria, he could not as an artist afford to give way to it.

Among painters, Gauguin probably offers the best comparison. The Tahitian scene, with its 'primitiveness', its emotional slabs of colour, soft bronze bodies and palpable contacts, is not far removed from the plumed serpents and river-bathers of Mexico.

II

The search for the primitive and for sex—he begins by being the lyrical poet of sex, and ends by being its prophet; and there, roughly, is the good and bad of Lawrence. Apart from this illumination and obsession, half-making and half-wrecking his art, there is the detached artist of the first half of *Sons and Lovers*, of numerous passages in his other novels, of *Twilight in Italy*, a dozen short stories and as many poems. It is not the most magical part of Lawrence, this earlier, detached, and naturalistic self, but without it he would hardly have been an artist at all—certainly not a novelist.

Sons and Lovers, his third book, was published in 1913, when Lawrence was twenty-eight. He had been working on it for several years (it is an objective account of his early life), and had re-written many parts as often as four times. It is easily the best of his novels, and contains the only full-length character which Lawrence created in fiction—the portrait of his mother. With her death, he cut the ties from his family and his early surroundings and never really saw the objective world of human beings again except by the flashes of his own personality and sex. Mrs. Morel dies half-way through the book; the change is obvious at once. As the son be-comes lover, as he begins to realize his sex, the naturalism of the earlier part of the story gives way to a luminosity, palpable more than visible, which infuses character and landscape; Miriam, the girl he loves, is no longer seen vividly, but becomes rather the symbol of her sex—a room, with curtains drawn against the sun, to which the author goes in the hushed glare, at times to rest, more often restlessly moving and looking for something which is not there. The search, the interior exploration, has begun. The lyrical impulse of the prose is identified now with sexual emotion. And this tendency, shutting out others, grew stronger in the novels that followed.

So long as sex is the *means* of his understanding, and not its *end*, it illuminates, as in nature, with rare shapes and colours. But when he fastens on to the fact of sex, so that its appearances become mere symbols of the reality, his art suffers and becomes strident, ridiculous, or sentimental. Lawrence's reaction to the fact of sex, in his writings, is invariably emotional or rhetorical. This is seen at its best in some of his poems (Whitmanesque, Hebraic chants, with an added delicacy and glee), and at its worst in his novels, where so often the sexual theme opens out with a false appealing luxuriance from which there seems to be no escape for the author, his characters, or the persistent reader. Oh, the monotony of this rutting mood! It is there, persistent and repeated, from the early days of *Virgin Youth* to the consummating sex-chant of *Lady Chatterley's Lover*; the same adolescent yearning, with or without its object, becoming cosmic. 'The same cry from the tortoise as from Christ, the Osiris-cry of abandonment'—so we are given a sex-crucified tortoise and a risen Lord who comes back to retrieve his defeat in copulation. This final 'religious' phase of Lawrence's art (*The Man Who Died* after *Lady Chatterley's Lover*), the mystical expression of the loneliness he found beyond sex, seems to me grotesque and sentimental in a way which his paganism or lyrical animalism rarely is. So long as he is chanting the praises of the body and seeking the fulfilment of physical contacts, his art can produce vivid and exquisite flashes: when he emerges to a sense of his final loneliness, he can only cover his failure by proclaiming this kinship of all living creatures in their sex, and in the common isolation which not even the act of sex can break down. Christ's despairing cry becomes one with the 'last faint coition-yell' of the tortoise. This is a levelling belief for a novelist to hold, since it pulls down his human characters as much as it illuminates his landscape. And in all Lawrence's novels—except, as I have pointed out, in *Sons and Lovers*—it will be found that he has not so much created characters as struck a new level of character. His people are alive, but in a submerged world, the notation of which is often blurred and confused. Their blood echoes an older instinctive life, they respond to the unconscious processes of nature round them, the seasons, night and day, and to the sex in themselves and in others. At moments, this life is theirs; they are strangers, husks of convention merely, walking heads, until the moments of recognition. They live on the impulses which in life only bob up now and then to the surface. Every one, for example, has at some time, sitting in a church, felt the impulse to pick up a hassock and hurl it at the preacher, but has kept still; and at another time picked up a pebble and thrown it into a pond, carelessly yielding to the same impulse. Lawrence's characters throw the hassock every time. Gudrun, in *Women in Love*, dancing on the island where she and her sister have moored their canoe for the afternoon, is surprised by a herd of cows, which approach and stare. She whips herself up into a corybantic fury and charges the herd, almost touching the horns of the nearest animals, so that they turn and run up the hill, where she follows with wild leaps and little cries. This is

Lawrence's way of expressing the impulses of a young virgin; by physical action. The impulse of sex in his characters is indeed unquenchable. In one of his short stories, 'The Horsedealer's Daughter', a girl tries to commit suicide by walking into a pond (it is the middle of winter); she is rescued by a young doctor who carries her up to his house, strips her, and restores consciousness by rubbing her with towels and pouring whisky down her throat. She recovers so quickly that within an incredibly short space of time she is displaying the physical passion and possessiveness which is Lawrence's symbol for the return to life. Such improbabilities are frequent; the sex-motive cuts across physical barriers, across differences of temperament and social class, with an instinct for the final coupling which blots out everything else from Lawrence's vision. He reduces life sometimes to a mere sexual shorthand: the hieroglyphics of the 'dark' life, man as a 'column of blood'. Lady Chatterley and her gamekeeper don't give a damn for anything except sex. So, in this sexual melodrama with a happy ending, colonel and gamekeeper meet in a London club, sniffing round one another like dogs, 'I'll bet you've got a good cod on you', etc.; the villain is an ex-soldier, paralysed from the waist down. As Dr. Havelock Ellis has pointed out, 'Lady Chatterley can never be happy with her peasant lover', but that does not trouble Lawrence, and they are happily married, to live happily, one presumes, ever after. Substitute 'sex' for the 'love' of the average novel and you have the essentially romantic outline of most of Lawrence's novels. It is, of course, a tremendous change; but Lawrence never worked out its implications, and it remains his central weakness as a novelist.

III

How much better are his short stories, where sex is implicit, than the novels in which it is displayed, worked out, and talked about! Lawrence can show the beauty of sex, the plumage and song, the first disturbing touches, with marvellous delicacy and ease; he can hint powerfully at the subterranean sex-personality in human beings which attracts and repels like electricity, the understanding between strangers. These moments occur frequently in the novels, but they *are* the short stories. 'The Fox' with its enclosed atmosphere and undefined male presence; 'Smile', which merely records the strange smile on the face of the nuns as they stand round a death-bed, and the smile, subtle, calm, and enigmatic, on the face of the dead person; in 'Wintry Peacock', the snow, the peacocks, the letter from the Belgian girl, the husband's 'Why didn't you kill that bloody bird, that bloody Joey?' and the mocking laughter down the valley—these are the glimpses of pure art in a world of strangers. I quote the first paragraph of 'Wintry Peacock' as an example of Lawrence's description:

There was thin, crisp snow on the ground, the sky was blue, the wind very cold, the air clear.   Farmers were just turning out the cows for an hour or so in the midday, and the smell of cowsheds was unendurable as I entered Tible. I noticed the ash-twigs up in the sky were pale and luminous, passing into the blue.   And then I saw the peacocks. There they were in the road before me, three of them, and tailless, brown, speckled birds, with dark blue necks and ragged crests.   They stepped archly over the filigree snow, and their bodies moved with slow motion, like small, light, flat-bottomed boats.   I admired them, they were curious. Then a gust of wind caught them, heeled them over as if they were three frail boats, opening their feathers like ragged sails.   They hopped and skipped with discomfort, to get out of the draught of the wind.   And then in the lee of the wall, they resumed their arch, wintry motion, light and unballasted now their tails were gone, indifferent.   They were indifferent to my presence.   I might have touched them.

That is exquisitely observed, and it makes a pattern on which the main incident of the story stands out with vivid boldness.   Lawrence wrote about landscapes and animals as no one has written before; sometimes, as here, with detachment, more often by identification.   Scattered through the novels and poems and travel-books, there are innumerable landscapes which seem to quicken on the page as one reads, trees and flowers which are living, sucking the water up through their roots.   Novelists before him drew their landscapes flat.   Lawrence had this ability of identifying himself with whatever he was describing—a larch wood, a turkey, a cloud like a macaroon—and the reader, for the first time

getting the feel of objects he has been in the habit
of merely looking at, is 'taken out of himself'
in a curiously heightened way. Perhaps it is
only a word that jogs the imagination: 'frost
face', for example, in the description of a mountain lion. Or an impressionism so vivid as to
be uncanny. 'The Mosquito' begins:

> When did you start your tricks,
> Monsieur?
> What do you stand on such high legs for?
> Why this length of shredded shank,
> You exaltation? . . .
> Queer, with your thin wings and your streaming legs,
> How you sail like a heron, or a dull clot of air,
> A nothingness.

Birds, Beasts and Flowers contains extraordinary
impressions, the free-verse taking shape, and
modulating from conversation to the rhapsodic
tone perfectly. This world of animate creatures
provided Lawrence with its own mythology:

But long ago, oh, long ago,
Before the rose began to simper supreme,
Before the rose of all roses, rose of all the world, was even
     in bud,
Before the glaciers were gathered up in a bunch out of the
     unsettled seas and winds,
Or else before they had been let down again, in Noah's
     flood,
There was another world, a dusky, flowerless, tendrilled
     world,
And creatures webbed and marshy,
And on the margin, men soft-footed and pristine,
Still, and sensitive, and active,
Audile, tactile sensitiveness as of a tendril which orientates
     and reaches out,
Reaching out and grasping by an instinct more delicate
     than the moon's as she feels the tides.
Of which world, the vine was the invisible rose,

Before petals spread, before colour made its disturbance,
   before our eyes saw too much.
In a green, muddy, web-foot, unutterly songless world
The vine was rose of all roses.

'We have lost something', says a character in one of the novels, 'which even the flowers have.' That, in its simplicity, was at times Lawrence's regret; and he could project his mood into the living shapes of nature with a sensitiveness and understanding which we never question. Human beings and animals in his stories are equally alive; a fox dominates one household, the stallion in *St. Mawr* is as vivid as any character in his books; the 'Evangelistic Beasts', hybrids, are more animal than human. Curiously enough, it does not occur to us that he may be anthropomorphizing nature; but we sometimes feel that he has made animals of his men.

IV

With all his gifts Lawrence failed as a novelist; certainly he is not a great novelist. The feelings of his characters are vague and inchoate, and the expression of these feelings (which are Lawrence's own) is equally shapeless, unfocused in the flow of his poet's-novelese. The crisis of feeling in his novels is often their weakest point—it will be followed by some Dickensian gesture on the part of the characters, which Lawrence, slowly emerging from the depths of the sub-personality, earnestly emphasizes. A bang on the head, for instance, is blessed because it comes from the instincts. He takes a tragic view of the ridiculous, because by identifying himself with the object he is writing about, he prevents himself from *seeing* that object, and is therefore incapable of finding it ridiculous. His utter subjection at times to his material, his reverence for the sort of ectoplasmic emotion which any object could draw out of him, can be infuriating: when he complains to a fish, for example, that it has no lips, no 'wistful belly', no 'loins of desire', and so he doesn't understand it. Yet in other parts of this poem, 'The Fish', his art is impeccable. Through his work there is a flow of sticky auto-biographical sentiment, never fully externalized, never properly understood by the author, which by its very proximity and warmth repels—as though one's hand had touched some viscid substance in the dark; it adheres to much of his creation. 'It seems to me', he wrote in the preface to his *Collected Poems*, 'that no poetry, not even the best, should be judged as if it existed in the absolute. . . . Even the best poetry, when it is at all personal, needs the penumbra of its own time and place and circumstance to make it full and whole.' This is true, and from the Rozanov-Lawrence point of view, axiomatic: literature must not be separated from life. But such a view demands an instinctive and undeviating singleness of purpose in a writer. And in Lawrence two strains, implying an artistic contradiction, are evident: the autobiographical—his sexual experience, which obsessed him and evoked a mass of undifferentiated feeling without any corresponding adequate form of expression; the lyrical—springing, it is true, from the same autobiographical soil, but requiring transplantation into other surroundings, the climate of a detached and unegotistic art. Lawrence's attempt to identify sexual with aesthetic experience is responsible for his failure as a novelist. It is in the outward flashes of his genius, in the brief form of short story and poem where his sex-mysticism has no time to develop, that his lyrical art achieves its best expression and is most truly personal.

v

Literature is not enough—that has been the final cry of the Romantic, new or old; neither, on the other hand, is life; and from the impulse of this double dissatisfaction there emerges the new figure. Some light is thrown on this attitude by Lawrence's criticism of Van Gogh. Two sentences have already been quoted; I give the whole paragraph:

I see Van Gogh so sadly. If he could only have set the angel of himself clear in relation to the animal of himself, clear and distinct but always truly related, in harmony and union, he need not have cut off his ear and gone mad. But he said, do you remember—about 'in the midst of an artistic life the yearning for the real life remains'—'*one offers no resistance, neither does one resign oneself*'—he means to the yearning to procreate oneself 'with other horses, also free'. This is why he went mad. He should either have resigned himself and lived his animal 'other horses' —and have seen *if his art would come out of that*—or he should have resisted, like Fra Angelico. But best of all, if he could have known a great humanity, where to live one's animal would be to create oneself, *in fact, be the artist creating a man in living fact* (not like Christ, as he wrongly said)—and where the art was the final expression of the created animal or man—not the be-all and being of man— but the end, the climax. And some men would end in artistic utterance, and some wouldn't. But each one would create the work of art, the living man, achieve that piece of supreme art, a man's life.

Well, Lawrence 'lived his animal', in the hope that 'his art would come out of that', and the result was that he fled from one corner of the globe to another, left Nottingham for Cornwall, England for Italy, Italy for Mexico, and back in time from Mexico to the Etruscan palaces. No reader in twenty years' time will be likely to take his Redskin games seriously, or see anything more than pathetic failure in a phallic pilgrimage which ended among tombs. His art to some extent has 'come out of that'; but Lawrence was remote from his ideal of 'creating a man in living fact' whose 'art was the final expression of the created man'—how remote, in life, we can see from the Letters and from memoirs by his friends, and in art, from his constant failure to achieve final expression. What a pity that Lawrence couldn't give up being a minor prophet and devote himself to becoming a major artist!

WYNDHAM LEWIS

WYNDHAM LEWIS is a hard nut to crack. As satirist, painter, critic, metaphysician, filibuster, literary dustman, and infernal dithyrambist, he is a continual affront to our sensibilities and a delight to the intelligence. The range of his activity, the mixture of astoundingly good and merely gimcrack, the sheer energy of his attack confound us. No other English writer to-day has been so badly served by critics, who tend unfortunately to write on the subjects that come most easily to them. Wyndham Lewis might well complain that though he has never hidden his light under a bushel, others have done it for him. But in fact he is himself largely responsible for the ambiguity of his position: criticism has not 'placed' him, and he makes the most of the escape. He is essentially a man of action whose actions take the form of words, a literary politician intent on effecting change, and hence he exaggerates his impact (this is what disturbs us) at the expense of his art. The genuineness of that impact, the superb muscular pattern, will hardly be denied; it is perhaps the chief delight of an author who eschews giving pleasure. At a time when knowledge generally is parcelled out in allotments, each man cultivating his own bit of garden and often enough raising a fortification round it, when every talent in the arts is trimmed into its particular shape like a privet peacock, Lewis sends his genius hurtling across a whole landscape, carelessly trampling and surveying the preserves of others. He assumes the free role of an intelligent man; his opinion on any subject he has studied—art, literature, politics, Shakespeare, human nature, the modern situation—is worth having and he gives it. While Eliot's 'I am royalist in politics, classicist in literature, and Anglo-Catholic in religion' only makes us grin, we are forced to agree or disagree with a sentence from Lewis's manifesto. In all his work he appeals primarily to the active intelligence; his criticism gives us the bones and sinews of his art.

As a critic, as the Enemy of countless books and pamphlets, Wyndham Lewis shows the human mind 'in its traditional role of enemy life, as an oddity outside the machine'. He reminds one at times forcibly of Shaw. In the first few pages of *The Doom of Youth* he gives this picture of an Oxford wine merchant addressing the 'youth of nineteen'—new style:

'A bottle of port?' (he would be careful not to say 'sir' lest it might wake the reflex responding to *seniority* rather than of social eminence: also, one cannot say 'sir' to a kid). 'A bottle of *port*? What next—a bottle of *milk* is what an infant like you should be requiring—it is the *dairy* you want, not the *wineshop*, my little lad!' Having paused to allow the pleased giggle of the 'youth of nineteen' to escape and spend itself upon the academic air, he would return to the charge. He would exclaim: 'What would your mother say if she could see you asking for port,

I should like to know? Still, I daresay it is for somebody a little *older* than you are, my little suckling. A bit of hospitality, what! In that case I shouldn't like anyone to say that I had taken advantage of a baby-in-arms and sold the poor kid an indifferent wine. So it's up to me, I suppose! I couldn't sell *an old hardened connoisseur like yourself*' (heaviest sarcasm and great sneers of infinite seniority) 'anything but this wine—and when I say it is 150 shillings a bottle, it is only that *for you*', etc.

Thus, he says, the up-to-date 'shrewd' wine merchant would administer his flattery. Would he indeed! Is not this another example of the vaunted Shavian common sense, the tables turned on life under the guise of exposing it, the rap over the knuckles administered by the schoolmaster giving us *his* 'slice of life'? Shaw's 'average man', Lewis's 'man of genius' are much the same person. Both possess an unusual amount of common sense which makes them feel invincibly immune against shams, and a perverse delight in giving it the fantastic twist. There are important differences between them, of course: Shaw is primarily a dialectician with a programme, Lewis a freelance artist: times have changed, and while Shaw regarded it as a duty to kick people into their right place in society, Lewis kicks them out of theirs. But each fills the role of traditional enemy, the public prosecutor of the ordinary man 'having his bit of fun', 'keeping the flag flying' in the good wind of popular sentiment. The attack on sentiment— especially sentiment about sex—is central for both.

The perversity of a thinker like Mandeville

which will pick out the discord from every harmony and find its pattern only in leaning *against*
the stream, has become with Lewis a mania for
opposition. Mind is opposed to body, will to
instinct, art to life. Shakespeare, in *The Lion
and the Fox*, is made Machiavellian; in Lewis
himself the adversary—vorticist, not-self, diabolical principle—rises triumphant. From this
conflict, or rather series of clashes, his art emerges
in the form of humorous explosion.

Satire is the one positive resulting from the
negative reactions of Lewis's critical temperament; instinctively he makes those reactions as
violent as possible in order that as satirist he
may give them the fullest release. *The Art of
Being Ruled* is thus in a sense the preparation
for *The Apes of God*; *Time and Western Man* for
The Childermass. If these books are read together,
in pairs, their relation will be obvious. Apart
from the intellectual backing or structure of his
satire, there is his faith in the virtues of the eye.
'Tâchez de devenir un œil,' said Flaubert;
and Lewis seems to have taken him literally.
What the eye sees is final—and ridiculous. It
opens a window for the intelligence on to a world
of Martians, whom 'the chemistry of personality
puffs up in frigid balls, soapy Snow-men, arctic
carnival-masks, which we can photograph and
fix'. 'The root of the Comic is to be sought in
the sensations resulting from the observations of
a *thing* behaving like a person. But from that
point of view all men are necessarily comic; for

they are all *things*, or physical bodies, behaving
as persons.' Here is the head of a minor poet:

In colour Lord Osmund was a pale coral, with flaxen
hair brushed tightly back, his blond pencilled pap rising
straight from his sloping forehead: galb-like wings to his
nostrils—the goat-like profile of Edward the Peacemaker.
The lips were curved. They were thickly profiled as
though belonging to a moslem portrait of a stark-lipped
sultan. His eyes, vacillating and easily discomfited,
slanted down to the heavy curved nose. Eyes, nose and
lips contributed to one effect, so that they seemed one
feature. It was the effect of the jouissant animal—the
licking, eating, sniffing, fat-muzzled machine—dedicated
to Wine, Woman and Free Verse-cum-soda-water.

The portrait (drawn from life) is exact and
vivid. More often, these heads—and the bodies
attached to them—are the monsters of a giant
movie seen from the democratic slant of the stalls.
Bestre, with his 'very large eyeballs, the small
saffron ocellation in their centre, the tiny spot
through which light entered the obese wilderness
of his body', is a fat boarding-house-keeper in
Brittany. It is only a small step from him to
the legendary Bailiff of *The Childermass*. The
court of justice of the next world sits.

With restless ceremony the Justice and his suite settle
into their places. . . . Jumping awkwardly from the litter,
which is brought to a standstill in the centre of the court,
the Bailiff approaches with a quick muscular step the box
in which he is to pass the rest of the day. Tapping on the
flags of the court with a heavy stick, his neck works in and
out as though from a socket, with the darting reptilian
movement of a chicken. His profile is balanced, behind
and before, by a hump and a paunch. He wears a long
and sombre caftan. His wide sandalled feet splay outwards as he walks at the angle and in the manner of a frog.
No neck is visible, the chin appearing to issue from and

return into the swelling gallinaceous chest. Bending with a birdlike dart of the head and a rushing scuffle of flat sprawling feet, he disappears into the back of his box.

Before the curtain goes up on Lewis's satire, he has first killed the actors with his diabolical eye, like the Caliph Vathek, and then galvanized them into action (slowed down for our greater enjoyment) with the electricity of an irrational life-force. *All* men, it will be noticed, are comic; and they are comic in action, because their bodies are machines which never respond to the demands of the mind. Is not this the revenge of Lewis, the man of action, on the circumstances which have made him an artist? The weakness of his satire is that he must first kill, before he can give life, that he must parade his characters as dead specimens, propped up from behind and knocked on the head each moment as his art brings them to life: the thug, the mysterious Pierpoint, remains invisible, and we see only the extraordinary life-and-death antics of his victims. The spectacle is unique in literature, a destructive legerdemain made possible only by Lewis's surplus of energy. But it contains its own antidote. Such satire keeps us in two minds: delight of the moment, disappointment in the long run. It operates in short rushes, and though the author may keep his breath, he exhausts us.

Now, I think that Wyndham Lewis is probably the best natural satirist we have had since Hogarth —I say this after re-reading all his books—but his art has the check I have attempted to define above. In sentences, in paragraphs, he can be simply magnificent: it is when they are strung together to the length of several hundred pages that we realize the absence of any real *advance* in his narrative. Any book of his is better to begin than to finish (remember the openings of *Tarr* and *The Childermass*), and when you have read it once, to dip in again at intervals. He is always beginning again—a new image, a conflicting argument is added at the last moment; he must slash and slash so that it blurs his line. The metamorphoses of Pulley and Satters in *The Childermass* begin by surprising us but end in bewilderment: their rapid changes of age, sex, hair, and countenance deprive them finally of existence altogether. This, it is true, is part of the intention of the book; but the *method* is self-destructive. And in the texture of the writing an imagery which illustrates his 'philosophy of the eye' results finally in shortsightedness—the flashing of too many bright lights near the eye. It will be found in all his work, satirical and critical, that while he writes from an unfailing source of intelligence—an intuitive common sense—he develops his ideas and images till they become obsessions. In *Time and Western Man* he is more obsessed by the time-philosophy than any of the writers he is attacking. In *The Childermass*—which ought, one feels, to have been his masterpiece—the ideas, the characters and their surroundings, and the imagery which expresses them, all develop the buzz of obsession.

The good and the bad in Lewis are therefore inextricable; he is one of those mixed artists whose defects will always drag down the reputation of the artist below his best level. He has probably saved himself by the variety of his work, and his choice of a variety of styles: one line of development, the mastery of a single style, would obviously have been impossible. In *The Lion and the Fox*, *Tarr*, *The Art of Being Ruled*, *The Childermass*, *The Apes of God*, *The Wild Body*, and *Time and Western Man*, he has produced a body of work unique for its immediate impact and possessing an energy, a quality of intuition, to which readers in the future will return.

STRINDBERG'S MIDDLE YEARS

I

IT often happens that the mature work of a great artist is overshadowed by his earlier performance, the qualities of which are less complex and more readily understood. Genius may be slow to develop; the public catches on quickly. Verdi is a striking example of such treatment, his best operas—the work of old age—being unknown to many admirers of his music. I shall deal here with the later Strindberg, ignoring his early life and art which are familiar.

Strindberg was mystic and neurotic. He owned worlds remote from the ordinary view and in him inextricably mingled. All his actions, his poverty, his demoniac religion, his hatred of women and sense of social inferiority—the outlets, if not the springs, of his life and art—were intensified by neurosis. It is impossible to separate his spiritual struggles from his obsessions, and their juncture is responsible for all that is strange, and much that is deep and original, in his work. The connection between his life and his art is so near that the critic is given a double view of the same incidents and their controlling forces.

To step from the pages of his *Journal* to the scenes of *The Dream Play* or *To Damascus* is hardly

96

so much as to change one's shoes to go into the street. The voice is the same, there is the same degree of intimacy and repulsion, the same frayed cuff, and volcanic calm. Examine any photograph of him taken between 1890 and 1910, read what happened to him in those years, what he wrote; and you will find portraits and happenings and writers all agree. Morbidly sensitive in life, he was as an artist fearless and strong, a giant if ever there was one, and so he could dispense with those masks which even the greatest artists have found at times necessary to the continuance of their art. There lies his uniqueness as an artist. His greatness consists in an insight into human character as searching as an X-ray, a marvellous dramatic instinct (so that his life seems almost to be shaping itself for the dramatic forms to which it will be finally conveyed), a vision that is realistic with a poetry of its own, and an experience of worlds as visionary as Blake's or the Book of Revelation, which yet never leaves the precincts of street or suburb.

His life, one may say roughly, was a succession of periods alternating melancholy and calm. A period might vary in length from a day to a couple of years, but its curve was always approximately the same: a few days or weeks of an intense floating happiness, so vivid and tangible that it would seem they must last for ever; then, the abrupt descent, months, years even, of racking and incessant gloom, when he suffered the tortures of the damned; and the gradual return to light—each experience of this kind more terrible and crucial than the last, each driving him nearer madness, and telling the strength of further faculties. Simultaneously from each experience his art gained immeasurably.

The crisis of his life, after which he wrote his greatest plays, occupied the years 1894 to 1897.

II

In November 1894 he was an exile in Paris, forty-five years of age, solitary, ill, and tormented. His second wife, an Austrian, had gone to Saxen to nurse their sick child, and though a few letters had passed, conciliatory, promising reunion, Strindberg's inevitable bitterness prevailed, and she had threatened to take out papers for divorce. In Paris he found the solitude and phantasmagoria of faces which only a large town can offer. He struggled alone, and the bitter hatreds and disappointments of his life took shape.

A few weeks before, he had attained the great ambition of Scandinavian writers—a play of his was being acted in Paris and was successful. Everywhere he had been fêted, applauded, interviewed. Yet even as he walked back from the station after his wife's good-bye, his happiness changed, grew exultant, free, ominous of the return to solitude. Women were the magnets of his life, and as the current turned they attracted or repelled. When he had work to do he retreated into himself. Now he was alone. In a small room in the Latin Quarter he began the first of his chemical experiments, to find sulphur in carbon—and after that, the search for gold! Almost at once his mood altered. 'I am born into a new world where no one can follow me. Things which before seemed insignificant attract my attention, my nightly dreams assume the form of premonitions, I regard myself as a departed spirit, and my life proceeds in a new sphere.' He withdrew from friends, and wrote a letter to his wife, flaunting an imaginary mistress, which caused their eventual separation. Alone, he commenced the search for gold:

At the beginning of July the house is empty; the students have gone for their holidays. All the more is my curiosity aroused by a stranger who has taken the room on that side of mine where my writing-table is placed. The Unknown never speaks; he appears to be writing on the other side of the wall which divides us. Curiously enough, whenever I move my chair, he moves his also, and, in general, imitates all my movements as though he wished to annoy me. Thus it goes on for three days. On the fourth day I make the following observations: If I prepare to go to sleep, he also prepares to go to sleep in the next room; when I lie down in bed, I hear him lie down on the bed by my wall. I hear him stretch himself out parallel with me; he turns over the pages of a book, then puts out the lamp, breathes loud, turns himself on his side, and goes to sleep. He apparently occupies the rooms on both sides of me, and it is unpleasant to be beset on two sides at once. Absolutely alone, I take my midday meal in my room, and I eat so little that the waiter pities me. For eight days I have not heard the sound of my own voice, which begins to grow feeble for want of exercise. I haven't a sou left, and my tobacco and postage stamps run out. Then I rally my will-power for a last attempt. I *will* make gold, by the dry process. I manage to borrow some money and procure the necessary apparatus: an oven, smelting-saucepans, wood-coals, bellows, and tongs. The heat is terrific, and, like a workman in a smithy, I sweat before the open fire, stripped to the waist. But sparrows have built their nests in the chimney, and smoke pours out of it into the room. I feel like going mad over this first attempt, my headaches and the frustration of my efforts; for everything goes wrong. I have smelted the mass of metal in the fire and looked inside the saucepan. The borax has formed within it a death's-head with two glowing eyes which seem to pierce my soul with uncanny irony. Not a grain of gold is there, and I give up all further efforts.

He quickly became ill, haunted by omens and fantasies wherever he went. One day a mastiff would bar the way to a friend's house, his only refuge; he would see a child sitting on a doorstep playing with the ill-fated ten of spades; figures would appear in the dead coals, in the shadows of the room and the patterns of cushions. At night he walked the streets:

I entered the Rue Dieu. Why Dieu, when the Republic has washed its hands of God? Then Rue Beaurepaire—a fine resort of criminals. Rue Vaudry—is the Devil conducting me? I take no more notice of the names of streets, wander on, turn round, find I have lost my way, and recoil from a shed which exhales an odour of raw flesh and bad vegetables. Suspicious-looking figures brush past me, muttering objurgations. I become nervous, turn to the right, then to the left, and get into a dark blind alley, the haunt of filth and crime. Street girls bar my way; street boys grin at me. *Vae soli!* Who is it that plays me these treacherous tricks as soon as I seek for solitude? Someone has brought me into this plight. Where is he? I will fight with him!
As soon as I begin to run there comes down rain mixed with dirty snow. At the bottom of the street a great coal-black gate is outlined against the sky. It seems a Cyclopean work, a gate without a palace, which opens on a sea of light. I ask a gendarme where I am. He answers, 'At St. Martin's Gate'. A couple of steps brings me to the great boulevard.

·   ·   ·   ·   ·

The fierce July heat broods over the city. I expect a catastrophe. In the street I find a scrap of paper with the word 'marten' written on it; in another street a similar scrap with the word 'vulture' written by the same hand. Popovsky [an enemy who had threatened him in Vienna] has certainly some resemblance to a marten as his wife has to a vulture. Have they come to Paris to kill me? He, the murderer, is capable of anything after he has murdered his wife and children.

The perusal of the delightful book *La joie de mourir* arouses in me the desire to quit the world. In order to learn to know the boundary between life and death, I lie on the bed, uncork the flask containing cyanide of potassium and let its poisonous perfume stream out. The man with the scythe approaches voluptuously and softly, but at the last moment someone enters or something happens . . . a wasp flies in at the window.

.   .   .   .   .

Have I lost myself in a dark wood? The spirit has guided me on the right way to the island of the blessed, but Satan tempts me. I am punished again. I sink relaxed on my seat, an unwanted depression weighs upon my spirits. A magnetic fluid streams from the wall, and sleep nearly overcomes me. I pull myself together, and stand up, in order to go out. As I pass through the passage, I hear two voices whispering in the room adjoining mine. Why are they whispering? In order that I may not over-hear them, I go through the Rue d'Assas to the Jardin du Luxembourg. I drag myself wearily along, feeling lame from my loins to my feet, and sit on a seat behind the group of Adam and his family.

I am poisoned! That is my first thought. And Popovsky, who has murdered his wife with poisonous gases, is here. He has copied the famous experiment of Petten-kofer, and discharged a stream of gas through the walls. What shall I do? Go to the police? No! for if I can adduce no proofs they will shut me up as a lunatic.

Vae soli! Woe to the solitary, the sparrow on the house-top! Never was my misery greater, and I weep as a forsaken child that fears the dark.

In the evening, I dare not remain sitting at my table for fear of a new attack, and lie on the bed without venturing to go to sleep. The night comes and my lamp is lit. Then I see outside, on the wall opposite to my window, the

shadow of a human shape, whether a man or a woman
I cannot say, but it seems to be a woman. When I stand
up, to ascertain which it is, the blind is noisily pulled down;
then I hear the Unknown enter the room, which is near
my bed, and all is silent. For three hours I lie awake
with open eyes to which sleep refuses to come; then a feeling of uneasiness takes possession of me; I am exposed to
an electrical current which passes to and fro between the
adjoining rooms. The tension increases, and in spite of
my resistance I cannot remain in bed, so strong is my
conviction: 'They are murdering me: I will not let myself
be murdered'. I go out in order to seek the attendant in
his box at the end of the corridor, but alas! he is not there.
They have got him to go away; he is a silent accomplice,
and I am betrayed!

He tried to make gold from baser metals, and
to find heaven in a world of Swedenborgian hells.
A horde of devils, witches, *doppelgängers* beset
him, bringing with them the landscape of hell
and a whole apparatus of evil attack and omen.
He was stabbed by 'electrical' currents which
made it impossible for him to sleep, and always
he imagined that he was being murdered.
Wherever he went, noises interrupted. He asked
others. Yes, they heard the same noises. Occasionally he met friends who were ill and questioned
them—their symptoms corresponded with his
own! 'You too', he would say to one after
another, and go home indescribably saddened
and yet relieved, to face the terror of the night.
After months of torment and nightmare, he
decided to run away. One Sunday morning he
packed his things and left the house early, saying
that he was going to the sea coast, but whispering
to the driver to take him to the Rue de la Clef
near the Jardin des Plantes. Blessed relief! It

seemed another Eden! He could sit for hours in the sunlight, looking round at the flowers, the summer-house, the walks, the open sky. Peace of mind came to him, a sense of deliverance and naïve poetic beauty; life began again quietly.

From Paris he went to Dieppe, Berlin, Saxen, and the small university town of Lund in Sweden. Later, he wrote of these years: 'The great crisis at the age of fifty; revolutions in the life of the soul, desert wanderings, Swedenborgian heavens and hells'. To these his life in Paris was only the prelude. He became visionary, mad, clairvoyant. He was never far from the lunatic asylum whose high red walls and stricken inmates horrified and bewitched him. 'Am I Phlegyas, Prometheus, Job?' he would ask himself as he wandered in the inferno-like landscape, the great pine woods, and lonely valleys, with huge stones in them like old men or demigods. At the end of these years of inferno his mind cleared. He spent a year travelling round Sweden collecting the material for a book on flowers (the Sunday morning in the Jardin des Plantes), and in the next two years wrote six of his finest plays.

III

I have indicated the nature of his experiences at some length because they give the curve of his life, and because they form the background of his masterpiece, the trilogy of plays, *To Damascus*. It may seem strange that experiences of this sort,

bordering on madness, should assist in the pro-
duction of a masterpiece or even allow of a lucid
description (note the lucidity and detachment of
the passages quoted); but in the transition from
life to art there are queer changes, and what
we call sanity, sane emotions, or sane thought,
if transferred literally to the page—but that is,
of course, impossible—would look as shabby, as
startlingly *unlifelike*, as a shopman in a window
of wax models. What is plain is that Strindberg's illness, in assaulting his nerves and brain,
evoked a fighting spirit amid scenery of inferno-
esque splendour. Experts are not apparently
agreed on the exact nature of his illness: whether
it was paranoiac, paraphrenic, or schizophrenic.
In his account of himself, and in the vision and
machinery of his plays, there are traces of all
three types.

The world of the neurotic stands out stereo-
scopically beside the flat photograph of ordinary
lives, three - dimensional, oppressive, horribly
living. Imagine a teashop corner, one shiny
table, a man sitting over an empty cup and a
crumby plate, and behind him a waitress leaning
on a radiator, the pale electric light coming down
on both. It is so ordinary, one of the many
clichés of existence, that most people, having
taken the scene in at a glance, would dismiss it.
But for the neurotic it may have some special
meaning, be a part of his nerves and blood, which
grips him like electricity; he would escape, but
the current is strong and he cannot let go; he

feels, 'That man, that woman, seated, standing like that, have an intimate relation to me which is terrible; it is not accident that they are here, *they know me*; see, the man has looked my way, the woman has curiously smiled . . .' So every detail of the scene may become part of him.

Look, again, at Van Gogh's picture, 'The Bridge of Arles,' with its fly-like figure half-way across a bridge in an expanse of canal, sky, and wooden banks; at his pictures of sunflowers and of a chair, a room, a table, and a pair of boots. They strike the average spectator as being very ordinary yet very strange. Their spell is much the same as the compulsive interest of his surroundings for the neurotic.

I have mentioned Van Gogh. He and Strindberg have much in common. Both were solitary, fundamentally ascetic, and at times mad or near it. The famous 'Night Café', which Van Gogh painted more than once and which seemed to him fundamental of his art, might be the scene for *There are Crimes and Crimes*. I do not mean that, though. As artists, they have in common a *texture of experience*, a feel of life, a realism of existing surroundings, edged by neurosis, which in their art takes the place of symbolism while often serving the purpose of symbolism. There is an astonishing passage in one of Van Gogh's letters to his brother: 'This evening I was at Pulchri. Tableaux and a kind of farce by Tony Offermans. I did not stay for the farce, because I do not like them and cannot stand the close air

of a crowded hall, but I wanted to see the tableaux, especially because there was one after an
etching, which I had given to Mauve: "The
Stable at Bethlehem", by Nicholas Maes. It
was very good in tone and colour, but the expression was not worth anything. The expression
was decidedly wrong. Once I saw that in
reality, not of course the birth of Christ, but
the birth of a calf. And I remember exactly
how the expression was. There was a little girl
in the stable that night—in the Borinage—a little
brown peasant girl with a white nightcap, she
had tears of compassion in her eyes for the cow,
when the poor thing was in throes and had great
trouble. It was pure, holy, wonderful, beautiful,
like a Correggio . . .' In Strindberg's plays
there is a corresponding grandeur of mean details.
Misfortune is shown in the discomfort of cheap
hotels, the delay of letters, the attacks of creditors,
and gossip of friends. The Hell scene in *To
Damascus* is an ordinary lunatic asylum. It is
thus doubly terrible, for one feels 'This is a
lunatic asylum, such as the one over the hill I
pass in the morning', and in the same moment
'This is hell itself'. The imagination is allowed
no escape. Strindberg, Van Gogh—they allow
the imagination no escape; their art comes
irresistibly full circle, closing the net.

The nearest parallel ordinary people have to
neurotic experience is in dreams (all neurotics
are dreamers). There, too, everything is ordinary
and looks strange, the personality of the dreamer

pervades a whole landscape, moments are pro-
tracted to infinity, there is the apparent solidity
and detachment of persons and scenery which a
change or movement in the mind of the dreamer
may suddenly reveal as false (like sunlight to a
sick person). This dramatization that goes on
in the head of a man asleep is one of the strangest
and most fascinating qualities of dreams. The
dreamer is unaware that he is inventing, events
happen round him, scenes startle and develop
as in life; he may wake with the feeling, 'I have
had a great experience', 'I have been living
through years', which will remain with him
through the day, chequering his mood like the
come-and-go play of sunshine, long after the
details of his dream have receded.

The connection between dreaming and artistic
creation, and even neurotic hallucination, is
obviously very close. In the life of artist, dreamer,
and neurotic, unconscious thoughts are continu-
ally on the surface, the imagination is bold
and independent. The artist perhaps exercises
control, whereas the dreamer and the neurotic
are controlled by their unconscious thought.

Now, if you glance back at the passages from
Strindberg's autobiography quoted above in
Section II, you will notice perhaps their resemblance to dreams (I did not choose them with
that object); the incidents might have happened
to any one—in dreams. The resemblance is
important, for the form which Strindberg adopted
for his later plays (*The Dream Play*, *To Damascus*,

The Spook Sonata) was a dream-form. A good deal of nonsense has been written about 'significant form', but one may say that the form of his great plays was significant to Strindberg who lived and suffered every turn of them. (The influence of sunstroke on the form of Van Gogh's later pictures may be compared.) Strindberg succeeded in expressing the *whole* of his experience, a rare achievement even for a great artist. He had no watertight compartments of his own ('the author in private life'); his experience directly moulded his art-form. One realizes the force of his assertion that 'the only fiction worth while is that which deals unreservedly with the author's own self', for what seem on the stage to be consummate pieces of invention were in many cases literal transpositions of fact.

IV

The crisis of his life found its final expression in a trilogy of plays, *To Damascus*. After the three years of inferno in which he wrote nothing except scientific articles and the *Journal* from which he drew afterwards for his autobiography, there was an outburst of creative energy amazing even for Strindberg. Between 1897 and 1899 he wrote the following plays:

1897–8 *To Damascus*, Parts I and II.
1898 *Advent.*
1899 *There are Crimes and Crimes.*

The third part of *To Damascus* was completed a few years later. The trilogy, which has never been published in an English translation, is admitted, by continental critics whose opinion I trust, to be Strindberg's masterpiece. I have been able to read a typescript version 'authorized by Strindberg' at the British Museum, but this contains only the first play of the three, and even so omits an indispensable scene. But it gives a wide enough glimpse for the reader to imagine what must be the effect of the whole play. There are few plays that have so impressed and moved me since I first read *King Lear*. *To Damascus* has the simple essential quality, the utter isolation of great art. What surprised me most in reading it was not its queerness but its sanity, not its obsessions but its profound spiritual depth. I began by saying that Strindberg was a mystic as well as a neurotic. *To Damascus*, in the realm of art, proves this magnificently. It is a morality play in terms of everyday modern life: *Swanwhite*, *The Dream Play*, *Legends*, and *Zones of the Spirit* in one; as bare and direct as Greek tragedy, with a dream-edge which is alternately enchanting and terrifying. It has caught, too, in moments of beauty the stillness of Sunday morning in the Jardin des Plantes. The scenes are a street corner, a doctor's consulting-room, a bedroom in a hotel, a sea beach, a mountain pass, a cottage in the mountains, a lunatic asylum; and back on reverse order through the same scenes. The Unknown, a middle-aged poet, meets a doctor's wife, whose name even he does not know, and he hopes with her to obliterate the sufferings of the past. He gives her a name, an age, a character such as he would wish, and their struggle—against his past life—begins. These two characters dominate the play, Everyman figures yet individual human beings.

The scene is realistic in its detail. This soliloquy is taken from the first few minutes of the action:

Unknown [*on a park seat, tracing with his stick on the ground*]. It's Sunday afternoon! The long grey dull Sunday afternoon, when the people have had their cabbage and beef, and boiled potatoes. Now the old folk are sleeping, and the young ones are playing chess and smoking. The servants have gone to evensong, and the shops are shut. Oh this long dreary afternoon! Day of rest, when the soul ceases to stir;—then it is quite impossible to come across the face of a friend, as to get into the public-house!

Act II, Scene 2 begins thus:

A cottage on a cliff by the sea. Table and chairs outside. The Unknown Man and the Lady in summer clothing, they look younger than in the previous scene. The Lady is crocheting.

Unknown. Three days of happiness and peace by my wife's side, and the sense of unrest returns.
Lady. What do you fear?
Unknown. That this will not last long!
Lady. Why do you think so?
Unknown. I don't know; I think it must come to an end, suddenly, terribly. There is something false in this

very sunlight and this calm, and I feel as if happiness does not form part of my destiny.

Lady. Why, but all is made up; my parents are resigned! My husband understands and has written kindly.

Unknown. What good is it, what good is it? Destiny is weaving her plot. I again hear the hammer fall, the chairs are being pushed from the table, the judgment has been passed, but it must have been passed before I was born, because already in my childhood I was working off the penalty! There is no time in my life to which I can look back with joy!

Lady. And you, poor husband, have got everything you wished in life.

Unknown. Everything, but alas I forgot to ask for gold.

Lady. Now you are dwelling on that again.

Unknown. Can you wonder at it?

Lady. Hush.

Unknown. What are you always doing? You sit like one of Parcae drawing the thread through your fingers—but do that. I know nothing more beautiful than to see a woman bending over her work, or over her child. What are you crocheting?

Lady. Nothing in particular, just to have something in my hands.

Unknown. It looks like a net of nerves and knots where your thoughts are riveted together. I imagine that your brain looks like that inside.

Lady. If I only had half the ideas you credit me with; but I have no ideas at all.

Unknown. Perhaps that is why I thrive so well in your company, and why I find you perfect and cannot imagine life without you! Now the cloud has vanished! Now the sky is high, the wind is warm, feel how it caresses one! This is to live; yes, now I live, just now! and I feel my being dilate, expand, grow thin as air, become infinite; I am everywhere, in the sea is my blood, the mountains are my bones, in the trees, the flowers.

So brief a passage gives only a taste of the play's whole quality, the sense of fate mixing with common life, the intense personal drama of the leading characters; and it shows hardly at all the essential dream-structure of the play. The premonitions, hallucinations, and obsessions of Strindberg's own life become here the devices of a pure and vital art. His apparatus for living, as I have shown it, could be a Heath Robinson affair, but for the purposes of writing drama it was marvellously compact and attuned.

English criticism has tended to dismiss Strindberg as a rowdy Titan, a 'henpecked Bluebeard' and Dickensian *fou*; the sort of man—suspicious of himself, his wife, the neighbours, the servants, the dog—who would scream, 'Janet, donkeys!' or surprise a visitor with the remark: 'At two o'clock I am going to be sick'. But Strindberg's suspicion of himself and others is itself so deep and visionary that beside normal insight it seems almost clairvoyant. Caricature in any case ignores his genius: the internal, battered, and wandering spirit, as distorted perhaps, but magnificently strong and real. Strindberg uses his medium with an intensely personal and living touch such as I can feel in the work of no other recent artist except Van Gogh. The only live movement in the modern theatre (Expressionism, O'Neill) derives straight from him. There has been no dramatist since his death who can compare with him, and how many could one find among the dramatists of the last two hundred years? That some of his plays groan with an excess of spirit, I am willing to admit; but that is a characteristic also of Beethoven's late quartets.

These plays—historical, symbolic, and expressionist (how few of them we have seen!)—are the living drama of Strindberg's spiritual adventures. They stage the conflicts and passions which he himself experienced, and are therefore one-sided; but this, so far from violating the dramatic form, expands it. His character was such that an explosion could split it at once into a number of component active selves, inevitably in conflict; and his life was made up of spiritual explosions. At different times he held every shade of opinion and belief about religion, ethics, philosophy, art, science, politics, and human nature. Very often these attitudes conflicted: his hatred of life concealed a love of it, his eccentricities went with an almost sentimental regard for the normal and ordinary, he was sceptic and Swedenborgian in the same hour. Outside his art, it would be fair to describe him as fickle and often even insincere; but with his art as centre, the effect changes and we find rather a nature that is kaleidoscopic, like a box containing a pattern of coloured glasses which the least shake will alter. No man was ever born with such a genius for self-revelation and for the discovery of new dramatic forms in which to project himself. Björkman has said that 'Ibsen gave more to the spirit of drama, Strindberg to the form'. Every one will agree with the second part of this criticism; but many of us now would deny the first. Ibsen himself acknowledged the superiority of Strindberg's genius. Both inhabited a world in which radicalism, women's rights, and the opposition of self and society were real problems: that world now is as dead (artistically speaking) as a doornail—Shaw killed it. Ibsen's are predominantly plays with a problem, and they have gone shabby. The door slams and Nora walks out—why not? The younger generation knocks to come in—but it is already inside. People are worrying now over the best way of dressing the characters in *Ghosts* and *The Master Builder*: ought not Ibsen and Shaw to be played in period? I think perhaps they should. With every visit one pays to *The Master Builder*, the characters grow smaller; while Strindberg's characters seem to expand indefinitely, and to arouse fresh curiosity; it does not matter how they are dressed. This is due partly to the fact that Ibsen *completes* his characters, he shows us their whole lives. Strindberg leaves his unfinished. But it is also due to a particular quality of Strindberg's vision, a greater and more bewildering spiritual insight which conceives human beings as travellers through space, yet tethered to their houses, their boxes at the opera and corners in a restaurant. That is what gives them an air at once commonplace and infinitely strange; that is the real conflict in Strindberg's plays, and not the cat - and - dog sex - struggle which we easily detect. The sense of movement restlessly on and on, which you will find also below the exquisite surface of Hans Andersen's tales, separates Strindberg finally from Ibsen. Spiritually and artistically they are poles apart. If the movement in one is of a wind endlessly in flight, the other is narrow and fatal as a whirlpool. No comparison between them can do more than exaggerate their difference.

HANS ANDERSEN

An incident towards the end of Andersen's life
has troubled biographers. His friends wished
to honour him with some public recognition, and
they had decided on a statue representing Andersen as an old man seated with a book on his
knees and surrounded by tumbling but attentive
children. They showed him the design. He
was very angry about it; he hated the 'toothless
old man', but even more the children. At that
time he was old and in bad health; and biographers wishing to preserve the legend that
Andersen's life was 'a wonderful fairy tale',
which it was far from being, discreetly omit the
incident or claim that Andersen was too ill to be
responsible for his sayings, while his detractors
produce the anecdote triumphantly as the last
outburst of a vain neurotic man. They said
that he wrote fairy tales and was ashamed of
them. It seems to me that there is a much
simpler explanation. Andersen was a man of
very sensible and delicate imagination, and what
annoyed him about the statue was no doubt
some blatant sentimentality which appears nowhere in his own work. Even a writer as innocent
as Andersen must have felt that the modern
author of fairy tales, no matter how great his

genius, would be classed by many people as a facile baby-talker and squinted at superciliously by fashionable novelists and poets. It is known that Andersen was hurt by the attacks of Danish critics, and probably he was praised by enthusiasts whom he would have liked to avoid. Writing fairy tales is too often on an artistic level with revived morris-dancing—the childish pose of an adult to amuse other childish-minded persons. Only a fine imagination and genuine artistic sincerity can save the author from pose. It was natural and I think inevitable that Andersen should have hated this cant of childishness.

Childlike he certainly was in many ways, but that is a very different thing. He had a child's enjoyment of simple objects and a child's delight in dramatizing them in a vivid toy-like world. His best stories are a marvellous interlacing of imagination and fancy, so that it is impossible to say where one ends and the other begins. There are no Barrieish appeals to the reader, 'Do *you* believe in fairies?', no conjuring of spooks, or forced whimsicalities; his trolls and talking ducks and china shepherdesses, however arbitrary, are as natural as mayflies in the sun. Andersen's world is *one*, and not a real world superimposed with fairy prints. You never question his details, any more than you question the notes of a Mozart minuet. And yet into this ballet world he pours an astonishing variety of humour, pathos, homely satire, diablerie, and moonshine. No one, except Chaucer in his

'Tale of Chanticleer', has written such admirably humorous domestic scenes in which the characters are animals. 'The Storks' and 'The Beetle' are perfect of their kind. The human sense of these creatures never jars; one is kept amused and satisfied with little realistic touches. There is an example in 'The Ugly Duckling' of Andersen's use of realism for the sake of contrast which is none the less appropriate and extraordinarily effective. The Duckling has escaped from its farmyard and is hiding in a marsh:

In the morning the wild duck flew up and caught sight of their new comrade. 'What sort of a chap are you?' they asked; and the Duckling turned to this side and that and greeted them as well as he could. 'You're precious ugly', said the wild ducks; 'but that doesn't matter to us as long as you don't marry into our family.' Poor wretch! He wasn't thinking much about marrying, as long as he could be allowed to lie down among the reeds, and drink a little marsh water. There he lay two whole days, and then came a pair of wild geese (or rather wild ganders, for they were both he's): they hadn't been hatched out very long, and so they were particularly lively. 'Here, mate,' they said, 'you're so ugly I quite like you. Will you come along and be a migrant? Close by in another marsh there's some sweet pretty wild geese—all young ladies that can say quack. You're so ugly you could make your fortune with them.' At that moment there was a bang! bang! and both the wild geese fell dead among the reeds, and the water was stained blood red. Another bang! bang! and whole flights of geese flew up from the reeds, and there was yet another bang! a great shoot was afoot. The sportsmen were all round the marsh, some even sitting up among the branches of trees that stretched out over the reeds. The blue smoke drifted like clouds, in among the dark stems, and hung far out over the water. The dogs went splash! splash! into the mud, and the reeds swayed hither and thither; it was terrible for the wretched

Duckling, who was bending his neck to get it under his wing, when all at once, close to him, there was a fearful big dog with his tongue hanging right out of his mouth and his eyes shining horribly. He thrust his muzzle right at the Duckling and showed his white teeth—and then—splash! Off he went without seizing him.

Andersen's realism, even more than his humour (which he considered the most important thing in his writing), distinguishes him from all other writers of fairy tales. His stories are scattered with lovely descriptions of landscape—note the precision of a phrase like 'the colour of red tulip petals held up to the light'. This sense of realism saved him, too, from the fawning charm which spoils most writing of this kind. At times he is near to sentimentality, but escapes it by a breath, leaving only the impression of uncloyed sweetness. Any one who wants to test Andersen's delicacy of balance and conceit should read the charming little story called 'The Elf of the Rose'. Andersen succeeds there in telling a commonplace story of human love and revenge by means of an eavesdropping rose elf. Every detail of it from the thrusting of the plucked rose into the breast to the last moment when the people stand round the murderer's body, saying, 'The smell of the jessamine has killed him', is the lightest, prettiest fantasy. I think that this is a good example of what Andersen, and no other writer, could do with fancy alone. In 'The Little Mermaid', one of the best stories Andersen ever wrote, fancy is caught up by imagination; the effect of a legendary remoteness is admirably conveyed. Re-reading the story I find it difficult to quote a short passage which gives this remoteness, a quality more of the story as a whole. But the description of the sea king's palace has a hint of it:

The big windows of amber stood open, and the fishes swam in through them, as with us swallows fly in when we open the windows . . . Outside the palace there was a large garden with fiery red and dark-blue trees, whose fruit shone like gold, and there flowers were like a flaming fire, because they were always moving their stems and leaves. The ground was of the finest sand, but blue like the flame of sulphur. Over the whole expanse down there lay a wonderful blue sheen. You could more easily imagine that you were far up in the air and could see the sky above you and below you, than that you were at the bottom of the sea. In a dead calm you could see the sun: it looked like a purple flower out of whose cup all the light was streaming.

Andersen could give a queer reality to anything. 'The Shadow' is at least as odd as *Dr. Jekyll and Mr. Hyde*, and as plausible.

The fairy tale has much in common with the ballad, and Andersen uses all the devices of pattern, of symbolism, of questions three times repeated, which one finds in old ballads and folk tales. His treatment of death and love is conventional. Journeys fascinated him, and they occur in most of his stories. He himself was always in a fever of hurry, travelling across Europe between Denmark and Italy, complaining that he could never go quick enough ('I should like to ride on a cannon-ball through the spheres'); and when he was obliged for any reason to stay in his native town, Odense, he lived at a hotel so that he could watch the visitors coming and going and enjoy the illusion of travel. The wistfulness, which in most of his stories is inseparable from their beauty, was a reflection of his own unhappy life. He was the ugly duckling—which never shed its last grey feathers. One can see from reading his *True Story of My Life* and biographies of him how intimate was the connection between Andersen's life and work. His stories were the passionate experience of his life—not the by-blows of a scholar's mind or the day-dreams of a mathematician. Many of them he heard when he was a child from old women in the poorhouse. He liked to walk in the grounds of a local asylum following the inmates and listening to their mad talk in terrified fascination. His father and grandfather died mad. Andersen fought through life against madness and the fear of it. Miraculously he escaped along the airy corridors of his imagination. A psychologist might make something of the recurrence of two insistent symbols in Andersen's writing: the symbols of *whiteness* and *escape*. The swan was to Andersen almost a symbol of life itself. He used as a child to watch the wild swans from the woods at Holsteinborg flying out towards the Baltic, their necks strained forward like pointers, and hear their weird bell-like cries. It was the same Andersen who later fled to Italy, Spain, and the Caucasus, eager and panic-stricken, and thinking of his beloved Denmark but dreading the return to it; the same who for years was in love with Jenny Lind, and whom she would soothe, taking his head in her lap and murmuring that he was a child.

FOOTNOTE TO VERDI'S 'FALSTAFF'

THERE is no need to stress the purely musical quality of *Falstaff*, which every musician now realizes. What is perhaps less generally acknowledged is the originality of method shown in *Falstaff* and other operas of Verdi, and the appropriateness of Verdi's music to express character and action on the stage.

It was possible once to contrast Wagner and Verdi, and to speak of Wagnerian 'music-drama' as being a development of opera, and, indeed, a higher form of Art altogether. It was possible so long as Wagner's innovations, musical and dramatic, were fresh and surprising to the mind, and so long as people were largely ignorant of Verdi's best music. Neither condition now exists, and the comparison with Wagner must necessarily be of a very different sort.

Even if we take an opera of Verdi's which is hardly among his best half-dozen—*La Forza del Destino*—the dramatic effectiveness and beauty of many of the scenes are striking. The libretto is a conventional and rather clumsy affair of lovers, dying curses, expiations, and duels, but it gave Verdi the opportunity of writing music as spontaneous and varied as any music in the history of opera. The scenes, which develop quickly, have sufficient contrast and activity for the music to transform them completely. As in all operas worth the name it is the music which is dramatic, just as in Shakespeare's plays it is often the quality of the verse which is most truly dramatic, and not the actions of the players. Verdi had this gift of writing spontaneous lyrical music which immediately expresses, with beauty and conviction, the emotions which the librettist has tried and failed to present. It is a mistake to imagine, as many people do, that Verdi took a libretto and merely strung together a number of lyrics with no thought of their suitability. It would be truer to say that he uses a libretto as Shakespeare nearly always used plays already in existence, and that the librettist in most cases matters little more to us than the author of the original *Hamlet*.

Verdi's music expresses character, whereas Wagner's merely labels the personages of his drama with 'humours' (in the Elizabethan sense), easily recognized, and with a scenic background rather crudely expressed by the orchestra. Much of Wagner's music is scenic, and not dramatic at all. If one compares what is perhaps Wagner's finest piece of music—the 'Siegfried Idyll'— with the flowery bird-warbling version of it which appears in *The Ring* itself, it will be seen how much Wagner's music loses in essence when he tries to make it dramatic, and what an elementary idea of drama he possessed. (Beckmesser's humour in *Die Meistersinger* is *opéra*

bouffe at its most obvious.) Even to speak of
Wagner's music as being 'psychological' or more
humanly expressive is misleading. Wagner could
express a mood, as *Tristan* from the first bar of
its Prelude to the end of the 'Liebestod' plainly
shows, but he was no more capable of understanding the interplay of emotions which we mean
by the word 'psychological' than he was of
making a good joke. His music is psychological
in the sense that Proust's writing is; he had some
of Proust's accessibility to sensations and an
added epic sense which at times cloys the
expression of them.

But in his great operas, *Otello* and *Falstaff*,
Verdi was provided with librettos which stimu-
lated his full musical and dramatic powers; the
adaptation from Shakespeare, it is worth noting,
was made by a musician, Boito. The characters
in these two operas—Falstaff, Ford, Mistress
Quickly, Othello, Desdemona, and Iago—are the
figures of great drama; they live, and are not
merely the puppets of a musical expressiveness.
The background is represented, musically, by
the singers as well as the orchestra; it is part of
them and not only descriptive and external.
The tempest in the opening scene of *Otello* is
evoked by magnificent sweeping piled-up choruses.
Here, again, the comparison is with Shakespeare,
with such evocations as Lear, thundering on the
heath, with the effect of Enobarbus' speech,
'The barge she sat in', and Caliban's 'Be not
afeared, the isle is full of noises'.

In opera, the tendency is always for the ear to usurp the eye; this is, of course, inevitable and right, since the music is all-important. Much opera is musical tableau (long stretches of *Tristan und Isolde*). Ballet is introduced into modern opera in order to supply the movement on the stage which otherwise would be lacking. Now Verdi is always careful to keep his characters moving. In *Falstaff*, the movements of immobility are there by intention, and they are remarkably effective—when Falstaff sits groaning outside the inn after his descent in the linen-basket, and in the last scene when he stands in the moonlit forest waiting for Mistress Ford. The rest of the opera is quick with movement, the busy plotting of the wives, the parade of Falstaff, the snatches of love-making between Fenton and Nanetta, who can get hardly a minute to themselves with so much that is important going on. The music is as winging and quick and fertile, and as buoyed with the spirit of comedy, as anything that has appeared on a stage.

Verdi *enlarges* the stage of opera as no other composer has done. Let me explain what I mean by a comparison. In Tchekov's *The Seagull*, Nina, returning to the house of the young poet who is in love with her, and talking with him, suddenly hears laughter in the passage. Outside, someone coughs: it is Trigorin, her former lover who wrecked her happiness. Trigorin does not actually come on to the stage;

but the moment is one of tension and fear, and it takes the imagination off the stage into other rooms of the house where Trigorin has gone lightheartedly, unaware of her presence. This device of Tchekov's which he exploits in many of his plays is an important one. In Verdi's operas we find much the same thing. Act III, Scene 1 of *Falstaff* ends superbly. Falstaff is seated outside the inn recovering from his misadventure in the wash-basket. The women go, having plotted to meet him in Windsor Forest, and as they walk away their voices come from all distances, parting, faintly mocking as they confirm the tryst with one another, dying away. All one sees is Falstaff sitting heavily over a tankard. I may mention the similar enlarging effects of the tempest in the first act of *Otello* and the trumpets in the third act, the sacred dances over the tomb of the lovers in *Aïda*, and the unseen procession of pilgrims in the second act of *La Forza del Destino*. Those who have seen the operas will remember countless other examples.

Of *Falstaff* I will say only one thing more. I am not writing about its music as music, but as music of drama and the stage. I will give an example, to me astonishing, of Verdi's genius in using musical themes which exactly suit the situation at the precise moment when they appear. It is well known that *Otello* and *Falstaff* were Verdi's two last operas, written within a comparatively short space of one another, when he was an old man. One might have expected some kind of repetition of the musical material, even though the operas are so different; but there is almost none. The one example is profoundly significant. Near the beginning of the last scene of *Otello* occurs the beautiful 'Ave Maria': its quietness postpones and emphasizes the terror of the scene which follows. In the last scene of *Falstaff*, at the same point of the drama, that is, immediately before the climax, Falstaff peacocks into the forest, rather wistfully. He stands at some distance from the appointed oak, meditating, and sings a soliloquy in monotone which suggests the 'Ave Maria' of the other opera. But what a change! The one is Desdemona praying before her death, the other Falstaff, a disturbed, moony, and rather badly used lion! The differences between the two passages of music are not very great. And yet, from the circumstances in which they appear and from what has gone before, they are utterly different in effect! Wagner was incapable of using music dramatically as it is used here. It is typical of Verdi's greatness as an operatic composer that, again and again in his best operas, the music is not only identified with the situation, but suddenly quickens and transfigures it. Verdi's is the opera of poetry, Wagner's of prose.

THE INTIMATE JOURNAL

AUTHORS keep journals for various reasons; most of them, I suppose, from the same instinct which makes people side-glance at their reflections in shop windows. I have seen a man in a restaurant —an elegant young Jew—engaged in making himself as irresistible as he could to the woman seated beside him; and all the time he was looking past her at his image on the wall. Every smirk and slant of the eye was met in that stare in the mirror. He could see that he was getting on well. Now and then his gaze (in the mirror, of course) would wander to the other tables in the restaurant, appraising the women and criticizing the men, but it always returned to itself. What a much better view he had in the glass than out of it—everything there with the addition of himself! Obviously a more complete picture. I should think that a good deal of his contentment in life depended on his being able constantly to get a good view of himself. It was not enough for him to see someone else responding to his attentions: he must watch himself awakening that response.

So there is a type of author who needs the reflection of a diary. Events may be thrilling or important in his life, but he only gets the last satisfaction from them when they show up well on the page. Amiel, Marie Bashkirtseff, Barbellion, have made an art of the written confessions which played a natural part in the private life of a great writer like Tolstoy. 'I see myself', said Amiel, '*sub specie aeternitatis*.' That is a long way from the diary of events or social encounters and from a book like Pepys's which is natural gossip. The other diarists I have mentioned are passionately interested in themselves—and aware of it. In any situation they tap themselves as they would tap a barometer; the needle wavers to 'storm' or 'fair' and they are delighted. How the smallest happening can take on importance in an atmosphere so impregnated with personal awareness! There is a strange exultance in these intimate journals, a gushing centre of flame, like the hoarse naphtha lamp lighting the jostlers at a fair. It is somehow intense and urgently unreal, a dreamlike distortion of close-up views. An average man does not experience so strained and continuous a flow of personal experience unless he is under the influence of drugs or illness. (Note that all three of these diarists — Amiel, Bashkirtseff, Barbellion — were invalids; Barbellion was desperately ill. It is a common experience of illness that the patient is sucked down into himself; yet in his introspection he is capable of a greater personal detachment than he ever was before.) Self-contemplation can start the strangest of fantasies. Marie Bashkirtseff imagines how she will look in her coffin, the pale figure and the flowers set out in candlelight. Death is a constant theme, it thrills and excites above all others, for when death comes the possibility of examining it will be gone.

To such a person, whether the victim of an incurable illness or not, life becomes less a matter of experience than experiment. Hence the cool awareness in a writer like Barbellion of himself— the puppet to be dangled! He is 'different' from other people, less cautious, more aware. Barbellion writes: 'My life as it unrolls itself day by day is a source of constant amazement, delight, and pain. I can think of no more interesting volume than a detailed, intimate psychological history of my own life'. His own life is interesting to him—that is his first thought; the determination to make it public—much though he wished it—comes second.

The Journal of a Disappointed Man, a realistic self-portrait 'in the nude', was published in 1919. The truth is always shocking to some people (watch the face of an inexperienced person confronted with one of Rembrandt's self-portraits), and this shrinking attitude was particularly common in the first years after the war, when the *Journal* made a sensation 'in literary circles', but hardly penetrated to an outside world beginning to face the realities of peace. Now, attitudes have largely changed—even attitudes to literature. Barbellion has been dead fourteen years, so that the revelation of reading his book is safely posthumous, and the shock less. Rather, this

Journal gives us a series of small running thrills, such as we get from a shock-battery used by schoolboys: the reader holds on, grinning with new energy, a little afraid—afraid, too, of letting go! I do not think any one could read the book without excitement. Whether you sympathize with the author or not, he keeps you tingling and surprised.

He started to keep a diary at the age of twelve; and when he died in 1919, at the age of thirty, it had run to twenty large volumes of manuscript, from which he made selections for his books. By profession he was an entomologist, and held a post at the Natural History Museum. His sensitiveness and ill-health, as well as a quick imagination and terrific energy, were responsible for his writing. 'I fall back on this *Journal*', he wrote, 'as some other poor devil takes to drink.' As he grew older and an early death became obvious, he lived more and more in the pages of his diary. He constantly re-read and corrected his old diaries, convinced that he had written a remarkable book, and kept two copies, one at the bank and the other at home in a box marked 'One guinea will be paid to any one who, in case of danger from fire, saves it from damage or loss'. His life, and even his illness, fascinated him. With an irony which he fully appreciated, the *Journal* began by complaining that he is not really ill, only always 'below par'—so that he cannot effectively strike attitudes! When it ends he is paralysed in bed, relying on a nurse to uncross his legs before leaving him for the night. There is a hint of pose in his unhappiness, genuine though it was. He reads Lermontov or Marie Bashkirtseff, and seems to exclaim, 'I am like these: I, too, am young, unhappy, ill'. He expresses several times a wish that he may die 'artistically', like Hedda Gabler; and the *Journal* ends after a fine defiant passage with the words, 'Barbellion died on December 31'; which he wrote himself, outliving that date by six months.

But this is a small part of his character. His attitudes were deliberate, and he took an ironical delight in observing them. Few men have been more self-critical or detached; he examined a new emotion as coolly as if he were dissecting a frog—which saved him from morbidity—and yet he did not for a moment become inhuman in the process. He was his best critic.

In *A Last Diary* he anatomizes his writing and discovers these elements: (1) Ambition, (2) Reflections on Death, (3) Intellectual Curiosity, (4) Self-consciousness, (5) Self-introspection, (6) Zest of Living, (7) Humour, (8) Shamelessness. If we add to these his honesty and beautiful descriptions of nature and the charm of an agile, pirouetting prose, the list is pretty complete. Yet it still gives a poor idea of the disconcerting *gaiety* of his work: the odd jumble of landscapes, London streets, clowning dialogues, people quickly and humorously sketched, bits of criticism, tender, silly little love-scenes, a dismal reflection ending in a yawn or a cackle. The jog-trot of

the diary is singularly vivid.   Here, for example,
is a visit to a concert:

Arrived at Queen's Hall in time for Pachmann's recital
at 3.15. . . . As usual, he kept us waiting ten minutes.
Then a short, fat, middle-aged man strolled casually on
to the platform and everyone clapped violently—so it was
Pachmann: a dirty, greasy-looking fellow with long hair
of dirty gray colour, reaching down to his shoulders, and
an ugly face.   He beamed on us and then shrugged his
shoulders and went on shrugging them until his eye caught
the music-stool, which seemed to fill him with amazement.
He stalked it carefully, held out one hand to it caressingly,
and, finding all was well, went two steps backwards, clasp-
ing his hands before him and always gazing at the little
stool in mute admiration, his eyes sparkling with pleasure,
like Mr. Pickwick's on the discovery of the archaeological
treasure.   He approached once more, bent down and ever
so gently moved it seven-eighths of an inch nearer the piano.
He then gave it a final pat with his right hand and sat down.

It is the rare case of a diary in which the writer
has already done the sifting.   The everyday
scene accounts for a large part of his work.   His
life, except for an appalling string of illnesses,
was uneventful, very much like the lives of countless young men living in London.   In writing
about him the tendency is to exaggerate the fact
that he was an invalid and to ignore his admirably
sane detachment.   He was, it is true, bitterly
aware of his tragedy: the more happiness he
grappled to him—his marriage, the birth of a
daughter, the longed-for publication of his book—
the more agony it would be to die.   'A queer
man, drunken with wormwood and gall,' he was
essentially an experimenter in life; as it slipped
from him, though at the last he was resigned, he
found it a gaudy quixotic affair.

The author of an intimate journal, with all the characteristics of frankness, shamelessness, and a delight in self-revelation, is, like any other writer, a man with a mask. One of the first aims of a writer is to find a suitable mask with which to face the world; this struggle between the artist's personal character and the form his art shall take (his speaking voice, as it were) is indeed the most important struggle in his life. Only a great genius like Shakespeare seems to be exempt from it. Many writers—Henry James is an extreme example—make their style and then live up to it. His speech, action, and whole life must have followed that intricate style and point of view with comical closeness.

Now the intimate diarist tears off masks. He abominates any literary manner and even any general form of writing which can screen him off from his readers. He dislikes even the thought of writing for others to read, because willy-nilly that involves some kind of attitude on his part. What he does then is the exact opposite to the method of Henry James; James approaches life with a style, the diarist tries to shovel life into his work with no style at all. Needless to say, *some* kind of literary form must mediate between him and his readers, but he tries to make it as unliterary and inconspicuous as possible. His utterance must be direct, personal, spontaneous, unconscious, almost accidental. Logic, being formal, must go; when he argues, it is in gasps and short exclamatory statements. He must startle the reader by side-glances and a jumble of words under the breath; he expects you to eavesdrop as best you can. And here, if he is not too busily destructive, he must begin to realize that two contradictions are in the way of his being a writer. First, he wants to address an audience without addressing an audience; second, he wants to speak without, if possible, opening his mouth. The result is naturally an increase of self-consciousness and a somewhat inaudible mumble.

This may seem an exaggeration. Amiel is never cryptic or private in his writings; Barbellion—a much smaller and less serene figure—exposes himself lucidly. But in the end we have the intimate diarist for whom privacy is its own reward: Rozanov is the extreme instance. There is a sort of personal integrity of thought which can only be retained by making no concessions to the reader—let him read, let him understand if he can! So Rozanov gives us genius in the raw; it *is* genius—but at what a cost! He tells us that when he is writing he can believe in the existence of nothing outside his room, the hand lying on paper, the cat by the window: he might have added that he is incapable of imagining any one reading what he has written. My point in going for an extreme case like this is that here is a perfect example of a man looking at himself in a mirror. And he has the backing of a good deal of modern criticism. If the business of literature is merely to transmit as fully and forcibly as possible the personality of an author, why should he wrap himself up in plays, novels, or poems about imaginary things? That many critics consider this to be the function of literature is shown by the fact that they will treat a number of masterpieces as though they were only manifestations of the author, an over-flow of his personal life, and that they will put his private correspondence, his diaries and note-books, on the same high level as his finished work. The idea that every author is with more or less efficiency his own autobiographer, and that where he fails it is the business of the critic to fill up the gaps, seems to me fantastically wrong. Many people, no doubt, find more pleasure in reading Tolstoy's *Intimate Diary* than in reading *Anna Karenina* (more pleasure still in reading his wife's diaries), but they are not people seriously interested in literature. It might be a good thing if every great writer were as anonymous as Shakespeare!

The mask of the intimate diarist is a curious one. As I have said, the intimate journal as a conscious literary form began as an imitation of private confessions. Rousseau is the first 'inti-mate diarist', though his book takes the form of confessions. The diary brought with it that hush of secrecy so necessary in art as well as life to whispered confidences. It was to be confidential and yet broadcast, artificially careless, and an exultant self-revelation. To be done well it required a nice balance; it needed as well as the assumed naïvety of the diarist an actual lack of premeditation. *The Journal of a Disappointed Man* is a good example of a conscious piece of literary art in which this strain of unpremeditation is yet strong. I cannot think of any really successful intimate diary which has not some extraordinary quality altogether missed by its author. Samuel Butler's *Note-books* perhaps come nearest to it (no reader sees more in them than Butler did), but they are hardly intimate.

It is difficult to say where art ends and artificiality begins. Amiel is never artificial—the rest are. The danger lies in an art imitating life. Gauguin's *Private Journals* are entertaining, full of a vivid life, until one puts them next, say, to *The Letters of Van Gogh to his Brother*. Why is it that those letters, entirely free of art, are so terrifically moving? They are not well written, not written as an artist trying for the same effect would have done them. If it were possible to read Van Gogh's letters without thinking of his achievement as a painter, we should perhaps be less impressed. I am half-convinced, but still I should describe the *Letters* as one of the great masterpieces of modern literature. The definitions of art which insist that a work of art is the *conscious* creation of beauty would of course make a sharp division between Gauguin's *Journal*, which was meant for publication, and Van Gogh's *Letters*, which were not: the first is art, the second a slice of life. But any one who reads both books without theoretical preoccupation must realize that such a division is irrelevant and in the end utterly meaningless. There is no division in kind between the two; but only the difference, the colossal difference, between genius and the lack of it. Van Gogh's *Letters* are a work of genius:— not literature?

The attentive reader will notice that I have reached an opposite point of view from where I started. Criticism begins always by assuming that a work of art is in some way different from, and even opposite to, what one may call 'natural objects'. The letter written to a newspaper is a work (however inferior) of art; the servant girl's scrawl found in a ditch is 'nature'. That is the central problem of aesthetics—which the intimate diarist, trying to realize at the same time standards both of 'art' and 'nature', solves or bungles in a curiously piquant way.

ELIOT AND THE PLAIN READER

Plain Reader. Here is another book, I see, addressed to me,[1] the third in a few months: Joyce, Wyndham Lewis, and now Eliot: there is evidently a movement on foot to educate people in the post-war school. I suppose I shall read the book, if only to pretend afterwards that I have understood *The Waste Land* from the beginning, but I'm not enthusiastic. These straight talks on difficult moderns smack rather much of proselytizing. What do you think?

Critic. There is a certain amount of deceptive cleverness in them, of course, and the excuse of 'talking down' is made to cover the author's—and his subject's—deficiencies. But on the whole they are written honestly and with intelligence. Williamson's little book, like the others, is the work of an admirer. On the first page he thanks Eliot for 'the stimulus of his conversation', and you may take the book as expressing not only an admirer's attitude but Eliot's own attitude about himself. That is useful. I hope you won't be overawed. The book is also a pretty full commentary, and discusses ably Eliot's intention and poetic means—a lot of useful material has been pulled together from various sources, from

[1] *The Poetry of T. S. Eliot.* By Hugh Ross Williamson. Hodder and Stoughton, 1932.

the essays of earlier critics such as Edmund Wilson, René Taupin, and F. R. Leavis.

Plain Reader. You frighten me with names already. I object to this hierarchy of modern thought : poetry and criticism : damned little poetry and an ocean of criticism. Will you tell me why all this *explanation* is necessary? Isn't it the mandarin's substitute for apology and extenuation? Eliot's poetry seems to me—I speak ignorantly—a sort of Cromagnon skull from which critics have reconstructed a vast poetic skeleton which in fact exists only in their imagination. I am not used to such poetic reconstructions on the grand scale, which indicate, for me, not the presence of a new and great poetic talent, but a deficiency of creation, in the poet, and the gullibility or dishonesty of critics.

Critic. You must allow for enthusiasm. But there is something in what you say. Eliot is 'an exacting writer', he 'makes no concessions to the reader'—how often that remark is brought out triumphantly by the latest convert! Eliot's is a skeleton poetry. At first sight his influence may seem to have been out of all proportion to the mite he has contributed to literature. Like Byron, he owes his success to having impressed on people a new attitude. Byron's influence was Romantic and popular—it affected thousands of people who never read a line of his poetry : Eliot's influence is classical (but I shall have something to say on that in a minute) and affects, directly, only the few. Byron's is an attitude to life, Eliot's to literature, and through literature to life.   Eliotism is a minority movement, intense but small of radius, which yet has widening ripples.   Without knowing it, you yourself, as the result of reading and conversation, have to some extent been imbued with it.

Plain Reader.   What is this attitude—Eliotism?

Critic.   It is hard to define.   Eliot has described his point of view as being 'royalist in politics, classic in literature, and Anglo - Catholic in religion'.   But that doesn't help much: it is undefined and suggests merely an odd and unpopular congeries of opinions.   Williamson describes him somewhere in his book as 'an aristocrat writing in a democratic world'.   This also tells us little, beyond again emphasizing Eliot's aloofness.

Plain Reader.   Aloofness, yes.   That is characteristic.   In highbrow company now one daren't mention Tolstoy or the 'communication' of art. But I interrupt.

Critic.   To understand the peculiarity and force of Eliot's position to-day (I shall have to talk like a lecturer to get in what I want to say) it is necessary to go back a few years and recall his first impact on literature.   *The Sacred Wood* (essays) was published in 1920—note that he began his attack, like Shaw, with criticism; poetry and criticism have always been with him inseparable.   It appeared at a time when English poetry and the criticism of poetry were meandering in the pastures of a would-be pre-war country of the mind.   The war had temporarily

splintered English poetry. After the war, Jack
Squire's Country Boys were banding to put the
splinters together—(this, mind you, was the *van-
guard* movement of the time, apart from a few
isolated adventures) — to make the return to
leisureliness interrupted only by bad nerves.
(You find Eliot neurasthenic and odd, but look
up the Georgian anthologies, and read Squire's
poem about the little trout stream under the
floorboards in Fleet Street!)   In the emotional
relapse after the war this poetry was popular,
but it obviously corresponded so little with any
current reality or *tempo* of thought, that a change
was inevitable; this poetry in any case contained
the seeds of its own dissolution.   Eliot's sudden
appearance as critic and poet made the inevitable
change as abrupt as possible.   The attitude to
literature expressed in *The Sacred Wood*, the
attitude to life in *The Love Song of J. Alfred
Prufrock*, astonished and shocked by their hardness, definition, ellipticism, sardonic seriousness,
and a pessimism which, though often flippant
and dandiacal, yet had a curious twisted thrust.
It shocked, above all, by its maturity, for in these
books Eliot sprang at once to full stature as critic
and poet.   There was even an excess of maturity
('I grow old . . . I grow old . . .', written
at the age of twenty), a precocious weariness and
cynicism which suited the hang-over mood of the
generation that survived the war; and this, allied
to an intense if narrow erudition, at once caught
the sympathy (if that is the word) of the younger

intellectual set, who were without a leader. *The Waste Land* (1922) made Eliot's leadership certain. Probably those who came most strongly under his influence have forgotten, or never realized, how far Eliotism was imposed on them when they were at a loss, and how little it expressed any real attitude of their own. The shock of Eliotism was successful because it confronted the world of literature at a moment of low tension with a poetry the exact opposite of any poetry then current—the poetry of an intellectual, a Bostonian in exile, whose chief attempt was to reproduce in English certain effects of the French Symbolists, of Dryden and the later Elizabethans. It was an immediate capture by opposites. You will see in Eliot's own verse, when you look into it, that the *capture by opposites*, the surprising juxtaposition, the shock of contrasts, is Eliot's trump card.

Plain Reader. You are coming to his poetry at last. I find you have to explain, to explain, like all other critics.

Critic. It was necessary to recall the first effect of Eliot on readers in order to compare it with his position now. *Then* his poetry was acclaimed as revolutionary, surprising, odd, a psychoanalytic pattern 'as if a magic lantern threw the nerves in patterns on a screen'; *The Waste Land* then was a cinematograph of modern society and the human mind, for the first time agonizingly aware of itself. *Now* it is the classicism, the detachment and formality of Eliot's thought and expression, that is emphasized. He appears now as the *poet of tradition*, each word is answerable for in some earlier context, the stones of *The Waste Land* are comfortably cemented on to the edifice of the world's literature.

Plain Reader. This is new to me, indeed!

Critic. It may well be, though you will find it in Mr. Williamson's book, in the comments of the critics I have already named, and in Eliot's own essays from the start. How are we to explain the general change of attitude? Is it due merely to the normal shift of opinion towards an original artist which begins by delighting in his novelty and the surface surprises of his art, and only afterwards fastens on to deeper and more permanent qualities? With Eliot, partly. But his insistence on traditionalism reveals also his central weakness. He has written of the poetical function: 'The historical sense [is] nearly indispensable to any one who would continue to be a poet after his twenty-fifth year'; and, 'The historical sense compels a man to write not merely with his own generation in his bones, but with a feeling that the whole of the literature of Europe from Homer, and within it the whole of the literature of his own country, has a simultaneous existence, and composes a simultaneous order'. This refers obviously to his own practice. How does it strike you?

Plain Reader. I should have thought a poet needed not the historical sense but the poetical sense. However, I 'm not a poet.

Critic. The weakness I have just mentioned, but not yet specified, is indeed intrinsically poetical.   Eliot is the poet of attitude as opposed to the poet of impulse.   He is the great example, with Schönberg, of the modern academic revolutionary, the insatiable but barren experimenter with technique, the tame wielder of paradoxes; in Eliot's poetry, as in Schönberg's music, you will find a text for every possible modern experiment and influence, but rarely will you find true music or poetry.   In their work taste is raised almost to the power of genius; but it remains infertile, except in its effect on other artists. But more than that, Eliot is the poet of inhibitions, perhaps the only considerable poet who ever lived in whom the inhibition against writing poetry has been supremely powerful.   His mastery of this strange situation is indeed extraordinary.   Not to be free to write poetry, and yet to hint magnificently at it; to be the master of the final flat phrase, and yet to suggest new beauties, and obtain a new echo from the old ones; to come at the end of a movement (Symbolism), completing its decline, and yet to inaugurate a new movement in literature—to have done all this with a finality and finish which can be paralleled in few other writers, ancient or modern, is a very remarkable achievement.

Plain Reader.   You mean that his expression of the predicament of the poet in the modern world —the poet not wanted—is in itself enough to explain his influence and worth.   I can understand that poets and critics read him with avidity (his technique also excites them), but what about the ordinary reader (like myself) to whom the predicament of modern poets is remote and means nothing, just nothing at all?

Critic. The ordinary reader does not seem to come into it—except that it is *his* indifference which is in part responsible for the predicament. You can't expect poets to write freely in an age which ignores them.

Plain Reader. You can't expect readers to read freely a poet who ignores *them*.

Critic. It is a vicious circle. Eliot is a specialist. You may regard specialism in poetry as a mistake and an impossibility, and go another way; though I would remind you that an increasing specialism has been the tendency of literature since its beginning. Music, by far the most specialized of the arts, has long since discarded those moorings to life which still seem necessary for poetry; but that does not prevent music from being a language of art comprehensible to many people, and capable of expressing immediately the deepest emotions. Further, by its very detachment from ordinary meaning, music has developed a whole set of new meanings which are entirely *musical*. All arts evolve along lines which intensify and purify their effect: music becoming more purely *musical* instead of an adjunct to dancing and singing; poetry becoming more purely *poetical* and detached from common meaning and association. Eliot has said, I think, that a poem does not so much express an emotion as create a new one. That is the point. And I see in Eliot's poetry an attempt, heroic in its effort, to create a less personal, more purely poetical poetry. He has stated something akin to this himself, when he says: 'Poetry is not a turning loose of emotion, but an escape from emotion; it is not an expression of personality, but an escape from personality'.

Plain Reader. Eliot's poetry, then, possesses a theoretical interest, in which one may take pleasure?

Critic. Yes, and more than that. I. A. Richards has described the particular quality of his poetry as a 'music of ideas'. We read Eliot with an eye on the future, with the notion that out of his work a new poetry, more vital, more selective and intense, may spring. A phrase here and there hints the direction; I remember

> In the juvescence of the year
> Came Christ the tiger

> In depraved May, dogwood and chestnut, flowering judas,
> To be eaten, to be divided. . . .

That is perfect in sound, rhythm, and in its 'music of ideas'; it is startling and yet satisfies, it is utterly new to us. If only Eliot could often write like this! But of course it is a fragment. In his verse you will find these floating bits, the hints of poetry, which detach themselves and remain in the mind:

> On the Rialto once . . .

But the attempt at finished creation, at the

passage to set up against the achievements of the past, is stillborn:

> The Chair she sat in, like a burnished throne,
> Glowed on the marble, where the glass
> Held up by standards wrought with fruited vines
> From which a golden Cupidon peeped out
> (Another hid his eye beneath his wing)
> Doubled the flames of sevenbranched candelabra
> Reflecting light upon the table as
> The glitter of her jewels rose to meet it,
> From satin cases poured in rich confusion;
> In vials of ivory and coloured glass
> Unstoppered, lurked her strange synthetic perfume,
> Unguent, powdered, or liquid—troubled, confused
> And drowned the sense in odours. . . .

The fact that it is conscious pastiche does not enhance its value. One cannot be seriously interested after three or four readings. And yet Mr. Hugh Ross Williamson considers that this passage 'beats the Romantics on their own ground' and quotes Robert Graves as saying that a passage from Keats would appear pale beside it.

Plain Reader. This is really absurd!—Excuse me.

Critic. Eliot's devotees find a lot in his verse which might escape your notice. Let me give an example in Mr. Williamson's book. He quotes these lines from *The Waste Land*:

> O the moon shone bright on Mrs. Porter
> And on her daughter
> They wash their feet in soda water. . . .

It is an adaptation of a song popular during the war: Mrs. Porter is one of Eliot's seaside comics. Mr. Williamson's comment on these lines is: 'Mrs. Porter's eccentricity reminds us of another washing of feet, which took place on the eve of a Crucifixion'.

Plain Reader. You are making this up.

Critic. No—page 123 of his book. One expects these lunacies in any book on Eliot.

Plain Reader. You began by saying that this particular critic was intelligent.

Critic. So I imagine him. I can't dismiss all Eliot's critics as lunatics, or I shall begin to suspect myself. Perhaps then I should qualify Mr. Williamson's intelligence by adding that it does not extend to his reading of Eliot.

Plain Reader. Now you have utterly bewildered me!

Critic. Let us return to Eliot, then—the madness begins with him. I had broken off from a discussion of Eliot's 'music of ideas': I showed how he could attain it in fragments, and only *in fragments*, for that is his poignant endeavour.

But more often this 'music of ideas' is a crude clatter, with one key-change which he applies *ad nauseam*. The normal transition of his verse is from beauty to commonplace, depth of feeling to flippancy, poetry to conversation, art to life, the past to the present: in a word, the descent to triviality. The contrast may take the simple form of a poetic tag ironically set:

> When lovely woman stoops to folly and
> Paces about her room again, alone,
> She smooths her hair with automatic hand
> And puts a record on the gramophone.

The contrast here, graceful but obvious, is lovely woman—bored typist, Goldsmith—Eliot. But the setting may be more elaborate and capable of far richer effect:

The river's tent is broken: the last fingers of leaf
Clutch and sink into the wet bank. The wind
Crosses the brown land, unheard. The nymphs are
    departed.
Sweet Thames, run softly till I end my song.
The river bears no empty bottles, sandwich papers,
Silk handkerchiefs, cardboard boxes, cigarette ends
Or other testimony of summer nights. The nymphs are
    departed
And their friends, the loitering heirs of city directors;
Departed, have left no addresses.
By the waters of Leman I sat down and wept . . .
Sweet Thames, run softly till I end my song.
Sweet Thames, run softly, for I speak not loud or long.
But at my back in a cold blast I hear
The rattle of the bones, and chuckle spread from ear to ear.

A close examination of this passage reveals a continuous subtle interlacing of contrasted words and ideas. The beginning, which follows a beery good-night in a pub, is a cautious set-piece. The nymphs are introduced, and with line four the music is suddenly distinct (the line comes from Spenser's *Prothalamion*) like a theme announced in a symphony. Eliot's antiphony (mostly percussion) follows at once with the catalogue of picnic rubbish. The 'nymphs' return, this time with the 'heirs of city directors'; and so on. There are smaller contrasts embedded in the words which at the first reading one overlooks: the *silk* handkerchiefs, for example, among the bottles and fragments, all of which by a dignified gathering of speech become the 'testimony' of river nights. 'By the waters of Leman I sat down and wept . . .' is an obvious makeshift to help the return of the theme line: a Woolworth pearl set on the counter to distract while the jeweller's tweezers are picking out the real one! The last two lines are irritatingly familiar to readers of Eliot's verse.

Plain Reader. The whole passage seems to me incongruous.

Critic. It is. And yet note the effects obtained. The lovely Spenserian line, twice repeated and then varied, is marvellously set, its beauty is articulated in a way which makes it seem incomparably finer than in the original poem. Eliot's method here can only be compared with the habit common among composers of using an earlier theme for variations. This passage from *The Waste Land* is fairly typical of the poem's whole construction—the juxtaposition of images and ideas sardonically unresolved—and illustrates its weakness. It is, to begin with, synthetic and not fused. It depends on a series of anticlimaxes (and most of his effects are got by a variety of subtle and thumping anticlimaxes— a continual use of the For-she-was-only-a-water- rat method as a serious means of poetic modulation). It relies for beauty on the literature of the past (Spenser's line and the biblical paraphrase) and the archaic dignity of the nymphs, Thames, Leman—the life of the past. Eliot is a defeatist, *fin de siècle*—end of all the ages! Here as elsewhere he works on the assumption that poetry is dead, and that poems in the modern world are like old masters hung on the discreetly negative walls of a bungalow. He will not produce fake old masters himself, but in his pictures he will always hint at the past: their timbre, a corner here, a face there, sets old life jokingly among the modern dead. It is not surprising to find that he has half-confessed to this in lines remarkable for their austerity:

> Between the idea
> And the reality
> Between the motion
> And the act
> Falls the Shadow
> > *For Thine is the Kingdom*
>
> Between the conception
> And the creation
> Between the emotion
> And the response
> Falls the Shadow
> > *Life is very long*
>
> Between the desire
> And the spasm
> Between the potency
> And the existence
> Between the essence
> And the descent
> Falls the Shadow
> > *For Thine is the Kingdom*
>
> For Thine is
> Life is
> For Thine is the
>
> *This is the way the world ends*
> *This is the way the world ends*
> *This is the way the world ends*
> *Not with a bang but a whimper.*

It is one of the most remarkable passages to be found in all Eliot's writing; but its poetic value is negligible. On the musical analogy, this passage is mere meaningless *atonality*. The literal meaning is plain: of poetical meaning there is none. Elsewhere in the same poem we find a passage as good as this:

> Eyes I dare not meet in dreams
> In death's dream kingdom
> These do not appear:
> There, the eyes are
> Sunlight on a broken column
> There, is a tree swinging
> And voices are
> In the wind's singing
> More distant and more solemn
> Than a fading star.

Plain Reader.   That is the only passage you have quoted which I can honestly say I like without reservation.

Critic.   Begin with that, then. You will find other passages as good, and in time you will understand, even if you dislike, the cementing of fragments, the 'synthesis' at which Eliot aims. He wants, you see, to use the whole poetic orchestra—strings, wind, brass, percussion—which one hardly finds outside Shakespeare. In his strange, sweating, puritanical, bone-rattling way, he is trying hard to be an Elizabethan—a later Elizabethan. That he should succeed more often in capturing moods of Laforgue, Browning, and Henry James, is perhaps ironical. His 'period' is 1870. Psychoanalysis breaks up the period piece into odd fragments; the technique is new; the atmosphere old. You may have noticed that he always describes himself as being prematurely old, old at twenty, decrepit at forty. I doubt if this is affectation. As a poet, he feels infernally old.

I should sum up Eliot's contribution to literature (this is quite apart from his effect on contemporaries) by saying that he is the first poet who has worked consistently to obtain a *simultaneity of impression*: the fragment from *Gerontion* beginning 'In the juvescence of the year' is a good example of this. Other passages I have quoted show how easy it is to fail—and yet how interesting such failure can be.

Plain Reader. And shall I find all this in Mr. Williamson's book?

Critic. No, alas! You will find the exact opposite. He will give you Eliot as a major poet, *Gerontion* as one of the world's masterpieces, *The Waste Land* as the representative work of our times. He does not even suspect the obsession behind Eliot's reliance on tradition, his defeatist 'classicism'. Least of all does he suspect Eliot the academician. Still, you should read the book. Eliot has made him think. Perhaps that **is** the one thing in the future for which we shall all be profoundly grateful to Eliot. He has made us think.

WORDS! WORDS!

I

PAUL VALÉRY said once that he would never write a novel beginning, 'The duchess left her house at five o'clock'. And yet, how many good novels have begun like that! How many have driven the note home, on page after page after page, with an insistent drum-tap of triviality! All art hypnotizes in one way or another, and the novel without style does it by repeated banality, which the reader comes to expect as eagerly as he looks for the hero, the love duet, and the twinkling night sky. Banality seems inseparable from the novel, as it is from life. A good novelist of the second rank must be master of it, he must patiently nurse and satisfy his capacity for the banal—for how else will he be able to tell his stories and keep them lifelike? One cannot imagine an Arnold Bennett, a Zola, a Mark Twain without this capacity.

It is the life-blood, and the disease in the blood, of the novel. Let us admit its fascination! No other art provides us with such chunks of Life, such inventories of furniture, endless dialogues, reported events, and family-album photographs. What poet, sculptor, or musician would dare to attempt a *Forsyte Saga* in his own medium? Here is the novelist:

'Mrs. Braiding,' said G. J. 'That child ought to be asleep.'

'He is asleep, sir,' said the woman, glancing into the mysteries of the immortal package, 'but Maria hasn't been able to get back yet because of the raid, and I don't want to leave him upstairs alone with the cat. He slept all through the raid.'

'It seems some of you have made the cellar quite comfortable.'

'Oh, yes, sir. Particularly now with the oil-stove and the carpet. Perhaps one night you'll come down, sir.'

'I may have to. I shouldn't have been much surprised to find some damage here to-night. They've been very close, you know—near Leicester Square.' He could not be troubled to say more than that.

'Have they really, sir? It's just like them,' said Mrs. Braiding. And she then continued in exactly the same tone: 'Lady Queenie Paulle has just been telephoning from Lechford Hall, sir.'

From ARNOLD BENNETT's *The Pretty Lady*, opened at random.

This sort of thing can go on almost indefinitely in a novel. But the poet will make even a Caliban speak poetry:

Be not afeard; the isle is full of noises,
Sounds, and sweet airs, that give delight and hurt not.
Sometimes a thousand twangling instruments
Will hum about mine ears; and sometime voices
That, if I then had waked after long sleep,
Will make me sleep again; and then, in dreaming,
The clouds, methought, would open and show riches
Ready to drop upon me; that, when I waked,
I cried to dream again.

The difference between Bennett's prose and Shakespeare's poetry is more than the difference between a small writer and a great one, between minor prose and major poetry: it is a difference not of degree but of kind. Shakespeare's art is essential and extends to all its parts, so that we can quote a short passage from *The Tempest* which will immediately convey something of the quality of the whole, as, in a sense, the whole atmosphere of Wagner's *Tristan* is felt in the opening bars of the Prelude. But the extract from *The Pretty Lady* tells us nothing, it contains in itself *nothing* of the whole, and if all the book were like that it would be an astoundingly bad one.

We are so accustomed to reading novels with our minds asleep that the point of this comparison may escape notice. But if we look at the two passages again, and ignore the assumption that they cannot be compared, it will surely be obvious that although both employ words to convey something imagined by the writer to the mind of the reader, their use of words is utterly different. Shakespeare's creation does not end until every word has been tested for its contributory effect to the whole passage. Bennett uses words as counters; he is merely *giving us a report* on a scene which he has imagined, and there is no difference at all, in its effect, between his report and the report of an actual conversation which might appear in a newspaper.

Much novel-writing is reporting of this kind which leaves us at one remove from reality, i.e. from the writer's imagination; and the average reader is so used to this that any closer approach to reality is difficult, if not impossible, for him. He takes it for granted that a novel which he will enjoy must be easy-going, and must touch, without waking, the imagination. The presence of this dead surface—the novelist's 'report'—intervening between the imagination of the novelist and the imagination of the reader ensures a faint and easy contact. No hard knocks! Safely screened, the novel-reader is immune from the more difficult battle with Art.

I have suggested two separate steps in the imagination of the creative writer: first, the initial image or idea; second, its embodiment in words. The two steps may, of course, in the case of a great poet be one, or so interrelated that they cannot be divided. We know, for example, in music that Mozart's compositions came to him whole, with their full harmony, and once conceived they were remembered until written down. It is not unreasonable to suppose the same process in Shakespeare. With lesser artists one of the two tendencies mentioned above is likely to be developed at the expense of the other: *either* the artist's imagination will be strongest in its initial conception and will work, growing weaker, towards the surface of his medium (words, notes, or paint); *or* his imagination, weak to begin with, will work away from his medium, gaining more and more strength from the manipulation of the medium and the attempt at expression. Examples of the first: Berlioz, Van Gogh, Balzac, most novelists. Examples of the second: Chopin, Seurat, Gerard Hopkins, and many poets.

In literature the medium is *words*, and writers (except a very few) work imaginatively either towards words or away from them. Most novelists,

I have said, belong to the first class; they work towards words; the imagination, that is, is initially strong and independent of its medium— expression weakens its effect. Hardy, George Eliot, Dickens—the vast majority of English novelists. Their unit is not the phrase, sentence, paragraph, or chapter, but the character, the gesture, the scene, the denouement. They use words (insufficiently) to express character, gesture, scene. This is the type of novel to which the English reader is accustomed.

The second, and rarer, type of novelist works, like the poet, away from words; his imagination catches light from the act of expression; character, gesture, scene, emerge more strongly as one word in a paragraph suggests a better one, as the rhythm is amended or the sound improved. Sterne is probably the best example of this type among old writers; Joyce among the new. In the *Portrait of the Artist*, Joyce relates how, as a boy, he was taken to a hospital where medical students were working in a laboratory, and how he failed to understand the atmosphere of their lives until he saw, chalked on the wall, the word 'foetus'. The sight of this word acted so strongly on his imagination that immediately he found the scene familiar, and felt that he had been living among medical students all his life.

So it is from *words* that he finds reality, and *Ulysses* is such a search for reality from words. The tessellation of images is what bothers most readers who approach *Ulysses* for the first time.

Almost any sentence might be chosen to illustrate this :

Ben Dollard bulkily cachucad towards the bar, mightily praise-fed and all big roseate, on heavy-footed feet, his gouty fingers knakkering castagnettes in the air.

Most novelists would write :

Ben Dollard danced heavily towards the bar, red and satisfied, snapping fingers in the air.

Joyce's sentence is far more alive, and if it appears, isolated by quotation, as too heavily twirled, I would point out that it is expressive in its context, and that by such means Joyce has succeeded in building up a character which no living novelist 'in the tradition' has come near equalling. Preoccupation with words does not necessarily involve the substitution of sensibility for imagination or a weakening of reality. Since action has gone out of the novel, I do not see by what means the necessary movement can be restored except by action of the mind, that is, by an energetic vocabulary.

In his latest book, *Work in Progress*, Joyce pushes a great deal further certain tendencies of language latent in *Ulysses*. Three fragments have been published in England : *Anna Livia Plurabelle* (Faber, 1930) is the best and the easiest to read. I think that any one reading it carefully a few times should be able to follow most of the implications of Joyce's new language. But it demands a little effort, and if our attitude is merely 'Here is another good writer gone wrong', we are not

likely to get far. With most books it is possible
to go on reading in a steady drowse without miss-
ing much, because the author puts his words
together familiarly, and a cadence at the beginning of a sentence automatically predicts its close.
With Joyce, the cadences, the juxtaposition of
words, the words themselves are different.

Work in Progress contains a large number of
invented words, of words spelt in unusual ways
and compounded from different languages.
Joyce's intention is not so much to describe
things in phrases (the novelist's second-hand
report) as to harmonize the thing described and
the phrase in one chord—hence the need for dis-
carding familiar words and for creating new
words *which shall include the old words with a new
suggestion of what those words describe*. Thus,
describing a girl singing, he gives her a voice
'like water-glucks', and by substituting 'gluck'
for 'duck' and introducing several other phrases
like this for the sake of their musical suggestion
he enhances the description of the girl's song.
Other phrases from *Anna Livia Plurabelle* stand
out vividly in one's memory: 'a sugarloaf hat
with a gaudyquivery peak', 'owlglassy bicycles
boggled her eyes' 'she let her hair fall and down
it flussed to her feet'. I quote the concluding
paragraph, which shows how effective can be the
recurrence of a few simple themes working up to
a quiet climax. The allusions in these lines are
plain to any one who has read the passages leading up to them. Two washerwomen by the side

of the Liffey have packed up their tubs and linen
for the day, and as night falls, they are turned
into a stone and a tree, their last straggle of talk
coming through the dusk:

> Wait till the honeying of the lune, love! Die eve,
> little eve, die! . . .
> My sights are swimming thicker on me by the shadows
> to this place. . . .
> Can't hear with the waters of. The chittering waters
> of. Flittering bats, fieldmice bawk talk. Ho! Are you
> not gone ahome? What Tom Malone? Can't hear with
> bawk of bats, all the liffeying waters of. Ho, talk save us!
> My foos won't moos. I feel as old as yonder elm. A tale
> told of Shaun or Shem? All Livia's daughtersons. Dark
> hawks hear us. Night! Night! My ho head halls.
> I feel as heavy as yonder stone. Tell me of John or Shaun?
> Who were Shem and Shaun the living sons or daughters
> of? Night now! Tell me, tell me, tell me, elm! Night
> night! Telmetale of stem or stone. Beside the rivering
> waters of, hitherandthithering waters of. Night!

The echo ('Are you not gone ahome? What Tom
Malone?'), the drowsy lisp of 'my foos won't
moos' (my foot won't move), the yawning 'my
ho head halls' (my head falls), suggest the evening
and the deserted river-bank and the accents of
the women as they are transformed, better than
many lines of intruding description. Passages as
finished and distinct as this seem to be rare in
Work in Progress. Much of it is, at first sight, a
rollicking and unfathomable gibberish. But it is
advisable to approach this new book carefully,
as one would listen for the first time to a new
and astonishing piece of music.

For it is a piece of words as music. Whether
language is ultimately capable of the musical

extension to which Joyce attempts to push it (some of it is almost contrapuntal), I do not propose to discuss. We must have the whole of his book before it will be possible to criticize seriously such innovation. It seems likely, however, that we shall find some of his devices to be merely cryptogrammic, and others to be worth little except as a *tour de force*.

If, now, we put the passage from *Anna Livia Plurabelle* beside the passages, quoted earlier in this essay, from *The Pretty Lady* and *The Tempest*, we shall see at once that it belongs to the same *kind* as Shakespeare's and the opposite kind to Bennett's. It is a piece of imaginative creation in and through words, and not a report; it survives the test that a work of art extends to its parts and is to some extent contained in each of them. But Shakespeare's re-creation of language involves no obscurity, his inventions (when he invents) are natural and easily intelligible. Why then must Joyce put himself and us to such trouble by creating a polyglot language which may need years of study to comprehend?

Well, Joyce is not Shakespeare. He is a minor poet and a scholar who by terrific effort has produced one great novel, and is intent now on producing another, which will justify him *as a poet*. There is no question that *Work in Progress* contains poetry which Joyce has shown himself quite incapable of producing by the traditional means of word and metre. So far then he is justified. His privacy? Alas, that is constitutional, typical of the time; and it is the cost (apparently) that must be paid now for the attempt at great art. There is the lack, too, of any living language in the world to-day which corresponds with the Elizabethan spoken in Shakespeare's time: American comes nearest to it. Folk-poetry (such as Joyce's) must now be invented if it is to be written at all. A folk-poetry, with every one's lore in it and a music hitherto unheard in literature—what an attempt! The attempt merely is magnificent.

II

The painter dabs brush on canvas, the sculptor chisels stone, the musician draws his arabesques of balloons and ladders which are afterwards transformed into more mysterious sound. Still more curiously, etchers work with chemicals, cinematographists with camera and searchlight. The poet uses a common dictionary. *The public starts level.*

I was reading an article one morning in which this sentence occurred:

. . . Concerning that of which he speaks, the author is abundantly informed . . .

I read the sentence again (it occurred in the middle of a fairly intelligent paragraph), and then stopped, in order to pigeon-hole the style. There are as many varieties of the commonplace style of writing as there are subjects to expound.

A business letter is written on formula (*re* yours to hand), a love letter even has its typical short-hand whimsy. Obviously the sentence in the article I was reading belonged to the common-place, and it suggested the scholar's nook. My first impulse was to paraphrase colloquially: 'The author knows what he is writing about'. Then I saw that the sentence had shrunk, not only in actual number of words, but in some sort of dignity it possessed in spite of a well-worn absurdity. Surely, I thought, staring at the words, there is a faded grandeur in that, which my own version does not replace; *his* at least is a sentence, divided near the middle, with pleasant-sounding consonants, whereas mine is a quick graceless statement. So far as cliché goes, there is nothing to choose between the two. The words arranged themselves in blank verse:

> Concerning that of which he speaks,
> The author is abundantly informed.

So that's the secret of it, I thought; pedestrian verse masquerading as prose! And yet, though I could see the words now only in iambics, I remembered that I had certainly read them first as prose. I began even to doubt their triteness and cumbrous length. 'Concerning that of which the author speaks'—did it perhaps uncoil with a serpentine grace? 'Abundantly informed' —what could suggest better solidity of learning? After a few minutes of day-dreaming I could not be sure whether the sentence was verse or prose, eloquent or shambling, good or bad. The words would soon begin their 'grave morris dance' on the page.

Any pianist will tell you that it is hopeless to begin thinking of the notes when you are playing a piece of music, and that if you do your control will go at once. Reading is not so complicated a physical action as playing a piano—the eye merely picks out a tune—but even in reading poetry, when concentration is needed, it is fatal to think of words *as words*, and still more, of course, as combinations of letters. Fine lettering or illuminations shorten the focus of the reader, who sees the page under his eye but with difficulty beyond it. The Elizabethans who printed poems in the shape of hearts or crosses, and Mr. E. E. Cummings who writes to visual patterns of his own, are merely distracting attention from their own shortsightedness by helping the reader to discover his. It is perhaps natural that a writer who spends years of his life putting words on paper should develop an extraordinary sensibility to the appearance of words so that at times they assume a reality of their own. Zola saw faces in words. George Gissing noted in his diary: 'Yesterday I wrote for nine hours, and at last in that peculiar excitement in which one cannot see the paper and pen, but only the words'.

A child can hardly escape the fascination and arbitrariness of words. To write anything down is to give it a new value and emphasis. But this importance of the written word in itself hardly exists in a fully adult mind. Miss Stein goes on writing 'one and two' apparently with pleasure, but for most of us these words are too familiar and lacking in association to bear repetition. One might try over 'Popocatepetl' on a blank sheet of paper. Occasionally, poets who have written well have insisted on a magic quality in words apart from their association, but practice has hardly borne them out. A symbolist may set a string of words without logical connection in a poem, relying on the gem-like beauty of distinct words; but each word is valuable for an image or a sound, or a combination of the two. Maeterlinck's repetition of words, 'l'âme', 'la vérité', l'obscurité', like isolated chords struck on a piano, serve as starting-points for the reader, who goes off into reveries of his own. Whatever we may think of these literary methods, they are remote from childish scribbling. Poetry, it is true, must be read through a watchmaker's lens, but such magnification is the exact opposite of primitive speech, in which words also exist singly, bumping occasionally into others, like children that have not learnt to walk.

There is a surprising amount of 'play'—in the mechanical sense—between writer and reader. The medium of words can inspire fantastic imaginings on the part of the reader. Thus a word like 'yesterday' may evoke for the susceptible reader a colour, a mood, an entire landscape. Some extraordinary examples of day-dreaming over words are given in a book called *Creative*

Imagination, by Professor June E. Downey (Kegan Paul, 1929). '"Fortitude" does not call up the synonymous word "courage", but the picture of a mother singing quietly to her dying child.' Note the precision of that: the detail of the 'dying' child. Some readers anthropomorphize words, making the lengthy ones into clowns, and short ones into dapper men. Others allot them to different hours of the day: 'woodland' and 'vagabond' are given as early-in-the-morning words, 'kitten' as midday, 'melody' as a night word. One may be inclined to doubt whether any fully educated person indulges these fantasies, but the learned author of the book in question makes a confession of her own. She quotes these lines by Poe:

> For every sound that floats
> From the rust within their throats
> Is a groan.

And adds:

> Always after reading these words, I feel a dull ache in my throat, a dark green roughening, extraordinarily persistent.

Poetry then, like music, can have extraordinary physiological effects (a dark green roughening of the throat) on people for whom the author did not intentionally write: the *green* roughening imagined here is probably due to a suggestion from *groan*. Such irrelevancies, it may be said, have nothing to do with poetry or true poetic effect; but the fact remains that they play an important part in the average person's enjoy-

ment of poetry. Mr. I. A. Richards in his
Practical Criticism has shown that the standard
of intelligence and receptivity among Cambridge
students of literature is not very much higher
than what is displayed in the examples I have
quoted from America. That is, to say the least,
disquieting. What use is there in assuming the
'communication' of art when psychologists prove
by investigation that two-thirds of what a reader
understands from a particular poem is not
'communicated' at all, but invented by the
reader? The more 'simple, sensuous, and passionate' a poem is, the more chance there is for
a reader to project into it meanings and images
particular to himself. Art is perhaps a mirror
held up to nature—the nature of each individual
reader. Or it is the task of the artist, now he is
aware of the real difficulties of communication,
to develop a more exact and personal medium,
which will consciously exploit those overtones of
art which at present merely exaggerate the
difference between creator and receiver. That,
at any rate, is likely to be a belief on which
poets will work in the future.

NEW POETS

(W. H. AUDEN, STEPHEN SPENDER, C. DAY LEWIS)

FROM the cactus land discovered and solely inhabited by T. S. Eliot they emerge strangely on bicycles, removing ties, waving placards, and chanting inscrutably in native argot. We catch phrases as they pass: 'Take a sporting chance'; 'It's up to you now, boys'; 'What time's the train for No-man's-land?' and so on. But as our hearts rise or sink to these echoes, we notice with astonishment that the faces express something quite different: rapture, irony, surprise, rage, despair, high spirits, bad nerves—which is it? While we are wondering, the shouts die away and there is only the evidence of a thinning cloud of dust. Which, as pedestrians, we naturally resent.

Half a dozen small books of verse, two anthologies, here and there a manifesto—at any rate they have raised the dust.

In a sense it is the home-coming, the rejection of an exile which, prolonged, must have ended in sterility.

You that love England, who have an ear for her music,
The slow movement of clouds in benediction,
Clear arias of light thrilling over her uplands,
Over the chords of summer sustained peacefully;

Ceaseless the leaves' counterpoint in a west wind lively,
Blossom and river rippling loveliest allegro,
And storms of wind string brass at year's finale:
Listen.   Can you not hear the entrance of a new theme?

> DAY LEWIS, *The Magnetic Mountain.*

A new theme, or the return of an old one? Essentially, it is the return of the lyric impulse banished by Eliot; but an impulse changed by absence, queered in some ways and enhanced in others—'So this is England!'

The *isolation* of these young poets roaming the Home Counties!   A masonry between friends takes the place of expression.   Poems by Auden, Spender, and Day Lewis appear arm-in-arm; there's no separating them, no getting behind the everybody's-jargon in which they are interlocked:

> Woman, ask no more of me;
> Chill not the blood with jealous feud;
> This is a separate country now
> Will pay respects but no tribute,
> Demand no atavistic rites,
> Preference in trade or tithe of grain . . .

The sensibility is there, the nerves are queer; again and again you find this pokerface expression, the use of a Chinese alphabet of newspaper imagery.   The above lines from a poem of renunciation are typical.   Return of the lyric impulse? you may exclaim.   Yes, in spite of appearances, that is what it is.

Marvel at the design, the coils and bulbs, the receptivity of a good wireless set; then switch on the current, twirl the knob; you are in touch with the world of banality.   Think of these poets, then, as instruments attuned to such a world: the individual remains inscrutable.

> Private faces in public places
> Are wiser and nicer
> Than public faces in private places,

says Auden, and his is a very private face. He hints, often with beauty, at a mass of experience, of which his poetry is only the iceberg-top; we must guess at what is underneath. His difficulty is in bringing us as close as possible to this experience without loss of austerity and compression—essentials of his art. The nearer he gets to it the stronger is the impact of his poetry and the greater its individuality. But it does not get any easier. Some of his work reminds me curiously of Cocteau's opium drawings, the foetus-like bodies gashed at one side, the agonized stance of figures like living clusters of rawlplugs. Auden's is a poetry of the nerves.

Much of the difficulty, privacy, and exasperation of these poets is the result of an awkward transition. They form the wedge of a new forward movement in English poetry, of which Eliot is the master and Lawrence the hero. The difficulty of this change-over *in terms of Eliot* ('as though a magic lantern threw the nerves in patterns on a screen') to the position reached by Lawrence is immediately obvious. A personal, as well as a purely technical, obscurity results.

Auden is the leader, the compelling intelligence of the group, but Spender, I think from what has been published so far, is likely to be the best

poet. They all accept the consequences of
Eliot's attack on romanticism, his impersonality,
much of his rhythm and imagery, and a certain
clinching tone; no one reading Spender's *Poems*
(Faber, 1933) will doubt the strength of this
influence. The city which forms a background
of his poetry 'fixes its horror on my brain'; the
unemployed

> . . . lounge at corners of the street
> And greet friends with a shrug of the shoulder
> And turn their empty pockets out,
> The cynical gestures of the poor.

The note is recognizable. But this is no longer
Eliot's 'unreal city', with its simulacrum of life
and passion, its puppet crowd moving in nightmare sequence over London Bridge. The sentimental irony and sardonic despair of *The Waste
Land*, from which the poet found a refuge in the
past, have become for Spender the genuine hope-
lessness of reality and the present; there is no
going back, he says in effect, there must be no
pretence of dream or dovetailing of phrases from
older poets, for that is to escape the necessity of
the present. The images of life in a modern
city which haunt him with their emptiness and
urgency, engender despair and, at the same time,
express it. That is the focus of his poetry, and
to blur it would be to falsify:

> No, I shall weave no tracery of pen-ornament
> To make them birds upon my singing tree . . .
> There is no consolation, no, none
> In the curving beauty of that line
> Traced on our graphs through history, where the oppressor
> Starves and deprives the poor.

Such a vision imposes an iron austerity on a poet, and it is the measure of Spender's achievement that having made beauty wellnigh inaccessible, he yet often achieves it.

How? By the statement, first, of his difficulty (an excess of mannerism, a hint of 'attitude' would be fatal), by the statement of the body, of the 'love' of the poet for what he contemplates, and the hope of the future. It is here that Lawrence supersedes Eliot.

> Only my body is real: which wolves
> Are free to oppress and gnaw.   Only this rose
> My friend laid on my breast, and these few lines
> Written from home . . .

In another poem:

> Drink from here energy and only energy,
> As from the electric charge of a battery,
> To will this Time's change.
> Eye, gazelle, delicate wanderer,
> Drinker of horizon's fluid line;
> Ear that suspends on a chord
> The spirit drinking timelessness;
> Touch, love, all senses;
> Leave your gardens, your singing feasts,
> Your dreams of suns circling before our sun,
> Of heaven after our world.

Many of his lyrics are essentially the appeal of head to heart which will be found everywhere behind the writings of this 'iron' school of poets. It is the old dichotomy between intellect and instinct, made more acute by modern self-awareness, and exhibited in the sharp division of literature itself—Eliot on the one hand, Lawrence on the other.   I should describe Spender's poetry

as conditioned by Eliot but gravitating towards
Lawrence, though not towards forms of expression
in any way resembling Lawrence's. Such conflict and progression is, of course, dangerous for
a lyric poet, who, if any one, should feel free in
his blood to write; Spender obviously does not,
and yet he maintains a remarkable equilibrium.
Though the burden of *The Hollow Men* is there
('between the desire and the creation falls the
shadow'), he can fuse it into a lyric:

> Never being, but always at the edge of Being,
> My head, like Death-mask, is brought into the sun.
> The shadow pointing finger across cheek,
> I move lips for tasting, I move hands for touching,
> But never am nearer than touching
> Though the spirit lean outward for seeing,
> Observing rose, gold, eyes, an admired landscape,
> My senses record the act of wishing,
> Wishing to be
> Rose, gold, landscape or another.
> I claim fulfilment in the fact of loving.

It is the slow returning of the senses to a man
who has been ill; the acute delight and awkward
emphasis; a nostalgia for life itself. That mood
in its strength of despair or exultation is realized
with poetic integrity. At times a crude claim
is made out on a future. But here, I feel, is
a poet's real beginning.

THE MOVIE

IN a friend's house I noticed over the fireplace a painting of the Bois de Boulogne by C. R. W. Nevinson: it showed the curve of a road through woods lit up by a car's headlights. The picture was striking, bizarre, and yet familiar. I had often noticed similar effects myself driving in a car at night. Indeed, aesthetically, while there is small pleasure in going anywhere in a car by daylight, at night one gets extraordinary bits of landscape, the white road and the lit-up trees and black sky, delicate and nightmarish like a photographic plate. Frosty leaves and silver telephone wires, round a bend the dazzling ribbon of curb reflecting the lights of an unseen approaching car—all these, scratched in platinum on solid darkness, are attractive to any one who is sensible to visual beauty; and they were obviously familiar to the painter of the picture. I said to someone present that so far as I knew, Nevinson was among the first to see in these night illuminations a subject for painting. He replied: 'Yes; but of course it was done before in films'. For a second I was surprised; but he was right, and I remembered innumerable car chases in early films which must have contained pictures similar to that painted by Nevinson. They had not impressed me at the time, however, as being in any way original or beautiful. I asked myself, Was the fault mine? In a painting one looks automatically for some kind of beauty or aesthetic interest, but the vast majority of films do no more than entertain, and one scans them carelessly as one would a newspaper. Perhaps, then, in giving a rather one-eyed attention to the antics of people rushing across the screen, I had missed a bit of scenery worth looking at.

I tried to remember landscapes in films, and recalled a few hazily: I decided that the fault was the camera's and not mine. For one thing, in looking at a landscape in a film we try to imagine the original scene, and we think: 'How fine that must have been!' It is rarely that the picture itself strikes the imagination so vividly that we exclaim: 'Yes, *that* is magnificent'.

What obvious views have been made to pass as scenery! The same blank sky or theatrically massive cloud, the same pantomime sun dipping its rim hurriedly in the ocean, the same haloed apple-tree and quivering sprig of blossom! Consider the advantages which any film has over any play in the matter of scenery; there are a thousand details outside the range of the scene-painter's art. The theatre, for example, has difficulty with any scene that is out of doors. I have never seen a really good garden on the stage. Even the peep of landscape seen through door or window is usually unconvincing. And what curious limitations there are to the weather on the stage! How tired one gets of the bright, unfaltering sunshine and the whistling birds! They are all too much part of a situation. When the wind howls and a tray is rattled at the back of the stage, we know that the door will suddenly burst open and someone wearing a magnificent coat will rush in with a whirl of snowflakes as though pursued by a wolf. His first remark will be, 'It's snowing', or 'What a night to be abroad!'—something of that sort. The 'illusion' of the theatre is often a persistent reminder that we are looking at a stage.

In a film we could be shown a patch of sunlight on the floor, dimming and moving faintly away as it does when a cloud crosses the sun; we could look through a rain-blurred window at an umbrella tilted into the wind. It took fifteen years for film directors to realize this.

Pabst, Eisenstein, Dovshenko, René Clair, Walter Ruttmann, and a few others have learnt the effectiveness of *irrelevant* detail: detail, that is, which is irrelevant or contrary to the scene in which it is introduced. In all realistic art we find that individual emotions are set against the unceasing flow of an everyday world, in which a lump of coal falls out of the fire, or there is the distraction of a band coming up the street. Flaubert, as a novelist, discovered this eighty years ago, and Tolstoy made the same discovery, perhaps independently, twenty years later. I like occasionally in a film to see someone blow his nose; it saves us from the certainty that a handkerchief must quench tears.

The main line of development in films has been, and must always be, naturalistic. Two different ideas of film art are current. One is documentary: that films record actual events, whether in a studio or direct from life, and that the cinema therefore provides a document of modern life. The other, aesthetic: that film is a rhythmic art in light and shade, capable of pure and detached beauty, a visible music. But the director who logically works out one of these ideas to the exclusion of the other will inevitably fail as an artist; for, if he chooses the first, he will become a reporter; if the second, his pictures will be the movie equivalent of a page of Stein. Both conceptions are vitally important, but they should not be separated or opposed: one is indeed a development of the other. For the movie camera records, but it records in its own way, i.e. it does not imitate, but provides a new version of visible fact, which may itself be regarded as a moving pattern of light and shade, restricted in colour to the range from black to white, and in depth to the plane surface. The movie, for example, of dragon-flies will be less imitative in colour than a Japanese print; in depth, film and print will be about equal; in movement, the film will be more imitative than the print. And as the print, though in some ways a close imitation, can be a work of art, by its immobility, isolation, colour-pattern, and linear form; so the film, imitative in other ways, can be a work of art by its movement, combination, rhythm, and changing line. I have seen such a film of dragon-flies in which flash and quivering poise made rhythms as exquisitely as a piano piece by Debussy; and there is a film of the hippocampus which, though clumsily done, shows plainly what opportunities there are for an artist in these small sea and insect pieces. Here, then, is the *poème visuel* of the movie, the five- or ten-minutes' piece which is documentary in origin and artistic in effect. It is depictive, but it emphasizes rather the black-white pattern and rhythmic movement. From this to the 'pure' film, movement of lights and shades which depict nothing, is a comparatively small step; but we see, by comparing the best 'pure' films with even an inferior 'subject' film of the sort just mentioned, that the most skilful manipulation of light and rhythm loses much of its beauty when it becomes abstract; that, in short, the movie depends on what it represents, and, after a certain point, its texture is impoverished the farther it gets from actuality.

Between the documentary film and the abstract film we get the genuine movie, which has emerged from the first and contains in itself all the qualities of design and rhythm isolated in the second. The early films were all documentary: a scene was acted, the camera recorded; another scene, another record; and so on. The point is that these *records* were a grotesque failure —as visual reproductions of reality they were far

inferior to the worst sound-records made for a
phonograph; and it was the realization of this
failure by a few artists which led to the development of a movie art. The *silence* of the film—
that defect has been exploited to such a point
that one may say nine-tenths of the imaginative
reality of the movie has come from it. Another
defect, the poverty of photographic texture, was
responsible for all the developments of movement,
montage, 'camera - angles', arc - lighting which
are now the commonplaces of technique. It is
impossible, for example, to prolong a 'shot' of
anything—microbes, battleships, or a stage scene
—for five minutes without producing an effect
of such appalling flatness and inertia that the
spectator would become frantic with boredom.
The amazingly rich texture of such films as
René Clair's *Sous les toits de Paris*, Dovshenko's
Earth, and Flaherty's *Moana* has been attained
by the development of devices which compensate
for the flatness of the photographic image. The
camera, once a recorder, provides these artists
with a medium which is capable of full and
individual exploitation.

II

A real history of movies would be fascinating.
Three periods: the American slapstick, which
came straight from the music-halls; the German
cinéma intime; the Russian folk-epic.

Nothing remains now of the first, except

Chaplin and the new comics, Laurel and Hardy, the Marx Brothers.

The Germans created the first school of artists, chiefly under the influence of literature, and to a less degree of painting and music. Their experiments, apparently new in films, were in reality an extension of tradition from the other arts: *the film must take its place among the arts*—one felt that always behind the seriousness and over-heaviness of even their best productions. *Caligari* was a solid achievement in futurism (better than similar attempts in the theatre), but it was not intrinsically a futurism of the film. The Germans did many fine things, they created, rather too consciously perhaps, an art where there had been none before; but it was an art of the studio. Indoors, how strangely it was all indoors! Character, individual drama, the neighbourhood of tense faces, steep lights and shadows, the mysterious eyes that confront you, the dark figure in the street—they were all there, *in the silence*!

With the Russians, for the first time, we were amazed to see a huge expanse of sky, shining and fleecy with light cloud, below it a bare strip of horizon, and in one corner a moving speck, a man crawling remotely under the sky. Yes, for the first time we were really made aware of *size*. The so-called Hollywood 'epics' never gave an impression of size—no more, that is, than one gets from looking at a picture of the Battle of Balaclava or a panoramic postcard. But the

Russian landscapes were huge; the movement of men across a square covered by machine-guns, the train crossing the desert, the angle of the camera tilted up at a pregnant peasant-woman looking along a field—these were the vivid impressions of a new magnitude. The Russian film was naturalistic, propagandist, and *documentary*. In *Earth*, *Turksib*, *The General Line*, *Mother*, and *Storm over Asia* we have been given magnificent documents of Russian life. The faces of working men and peasants alone would make these films valuable. And it is worth noticing that the Russian film directors, whose object is to give emphasis to actuality, have made more technical innovations, and have produced more effects of pure beauty in their films, than the German school of self-conscious art—the only body of film-art that can be compared with the Russian.

III

At one time it was interesting to watch the effect of other arts on the film: what is important now is the effect of the film on other arts.

The introduction of photography had a considerable influence on painters of the last century: remember the racehorses, the Impressionist snapshots in bar and street, Degas's ballet girls; and photography itself was utterly unimportant as art. Any good painter had only to copy a photograph and his version would be an obvious improvement. But no painter or other artist can produce anything in the least like a film! Playwrights and novelists have tried a deliberate imitation, but how feeble the results have been! (*Street Scene*, *Grand Hotel* (novel and play), *Stamboul Train*, etc.). Movies have driven the theatre underground; it can't compete on their ground; the total effect will be, I hope, that playwrights will return with more concentration to their vital medium, the spoken word, for which at present the dialogue of trivialities is the substitute.

What has happened is that the movie has usurped the position of the theatre as the *theatre of action*: for melodrama the Saturday-nighters go to the 'flicks' and not to the local 'family theatre' (which in any case has become a movie-palace); Strindberg's ideal *théâtre intime* no longer exists except as a repertory-hall for the revival of old masterpieces, but there is a vital *cinéma intime* where good new work is always to be seen; the social drama of the present is to be found only in such films as *Kameradschaft*, *Westfront* 1918, *Earth*, and *The General Line*. Galsworthy's *Strife*, for example, is still being played in theatres, although it is out of date, simply because there is no similar play depicting post-war industrial conditions to take its place: Pabst's film, *Kameradschaft*, in fact has taken its place.

When we come to analyse the deeper general influence of films on other arts, a number of important facts emerge. I will summarize:

(1) The particular approach and quality of

movies, the 'momentaneity', is reflected everywhere in those arts where movement is possible, especially in literature.

(2) The freedom of the film-image from any kind of literary or historical association has provoked a distrust, among writers, of the conventional responses which attach to the use of words. The sunset phrases of the pre-war poet are felt to be unreal, because their glow belongs to the poetic genre, and a generalized emotion is evoked by generalizing words, by flashing jewels from the treasure-box of literature, rather than by immediacy and particular effect. So Gertrude Stein and E. E. Cummings (a far better writer) break up 'the family habits' of words, Joyce and the transitionists invent new words, and intelligibility is sacrificed for the particular effect. Such tendencies, though inevitable at the moment, are obviously dangerous.

(3) Film-art may be described as an impressionism emerging from naturalistic observation: e.g. the technique of *montage*, of assembling and juxtaposing images in a film in order to produce a visual and rhythmic whole, is naturalistic if each image is examined separately, but a sequence of such images is impressionist. Literature had reached a similar point of technique, independently of films, in Joyce's *Ulysses*. The interaction of the two techniques, in literature and film, will be important for writers.

(4) In movie there is no fixed scale determining the size of objects, and no agreed distance

between the camera and its object, the spectator and the figure on the screen. Within ten seconds we may be shown a woman's face so close that it fills half the screen, then the figure at fifty yards, or almost invisible at half a mile. This elasticity of size and distance creates in the spectator a pliability, an anticipation of the changing graph of vision, which results in a physical and emotional attitude quite different from that of the spectator in a theatre, where everything is fixed to one scale. There has been a corresponding loosening of distance in the scenes of the novel. Hero, heroine, fathers, aunts, cousins, butlers, and crossing-sweepers were at one time graduated carefully so that whenever one of them appeared the reader automatically imagined him at his correct size and distance. Such an event as a close-up view of the crossing-sweeper followed by a long-distance snap of the hero, one of a hundred persons getting out of a railway train, was unlooked for and never occurred. In the novels of Joyce, Wyndham Lewis, Dos Passos, Céline, and many other contemporary writers, the distance between the reader and each of the characters in the novel is liable to shift; the puppets do not move in uniform scale. Such alterations, if made too quickly or violently, are baffling, because they expect from the imagination a minutely *visual* attention which it cannot give.

(5) One of the most important technical discoveries of the movies was the close-up and, developing from that, the substitution of part of

an image for the whole of it. I mean: the picture of feet crossing on a pavement; a seagull and a masthead; a hat floating among drift-weed; cigarette-smoke spiralling up a window. Such devices (by means of words) have always been part of the technique of novelist and poet. Tchekov to a young writer: 'You must make them feel the moonlight as it glints from a fragment of bottle in the garden'. The exploitation, continuous and varied, of such devices in films has brought home their value afresh to the writer: he sees now their particular *visual* property.

(6) The *silence* of the movie has affected the *silence* of literature. Books—novels and poetry—are now rarely written *aloud* or read aloud. Thus, the voice of poet, or novelist, and reader is distant, felt perhaps rather than heard. It would be a shock for most readers to hear a modern poet reciting his own verses: Miss Sitwell's public readings have shown the gap existing between the written poem and the poem spoken by the author. This important quality in modern writing, produced by the absence of the voice in what is written, has been altered, deflected ever so slightly, by the far-reaching use of silence in films. I find it impossible to quote any clinching example of this, but every one who has followed carefully the recent developments of literature and film will be aware of its existence.

(7) The influence merely of the analogy between the brain's flicker and a film. Bergson has described the stream of consciousness as an

interior cinema. With or without knowing it, many writers have seen this comparison, and it has influenced their work.

These are not the sort of influences with which criticism usually deals. I have only hinted at their general operation. The importance of such cross-currents, at a time when no one art is isolated from the rest, will hardly be denied.